To Sam Stovall —
With best wishes to another
distinguished Stovall on his
way up.

Cordially,
Myron Kandel
Dec. 15, 1988

HOW TO BEAT WALL STREET

By Myron Kandel

BOARDROOM® BOOKS

Copyright © 1985 Boardroom® Reports, Inc.

All rights reserved, including the right to reproduce
this book or parts thereof in any form.

Boardroom Books publishes the advice of expert authorities in many fields. But the use of a book is not a substitute for legal, accounting, or other professional services. Consult a competent professional for answers to your specific questions.

Library of Congress Cataloging in Publication Data

Kandel, Myron.
   How to beat Wall Street.

   Includes index.
   1. Stocks—United States—Handbooks, manuals, etc.
2. Investments—United States—Handbooks, manuals, etc.
I. Title.
HG4921.K26 1985   332.63'22   85-14975
ISBN 0-932648-66-5

Boardroom® Books, a divison of Boardroom® Reports, Inc.
330 West 42 Street, New York, NY 10036

Printed in the United States of America

CONTENTS

Introduction vii

PART ONE
INVESTING IN THE 1980s

The Rebirth of America 3
How to Remove the Stress from Investing 11
The People Quotient 13
How to Identify Companies That Will Turn Into Winners ... 15
You Can Make Your Own Investment Discoveries 17
Be Ready to Seize Sudden Opportunities 21
Pick a Good Stock and Never Let It Go 23
Watch Out for Those Get-Rich-Quick Schemes 25
When to Sit With a Stock—and When to Keep Moving ... 27
Winning with the Losers—and Vice Versa 29
Squeezing the Dollar 31
Picking the Right Stockbroker 33
How to Unlock the Secrets of the Annual Report 35

PART TWO
ADVICE FROM THE PROS

Nine Lively Hints for Stock Market Success 51
ANN C. BROWN, *Chief Executive Officer, A.C. Brown & Associates*

Get in Early and Have Patience 53
LOUIS EHRENKRANTZ, *Director, Ehrenkrantz & King*

Fear and Greed Rule the Market 57
WILLIAM M. LeFEVRE, *Vice President and Investment Strategist, Purcell, Graham & Co., Inc.*

Wall Street Syndromes: The Triumph of the
Emotional Over the Rational 59
ROBERT H. STOVALL, *Senior Vice President and Director of Portfolio Strategy, Dean Witter Reynolds, Inc.*

How to Find Profits in Junior Growth Stocks 63
JOHN WESTERGAARD, *President, Equity Research Associates, Inc.*

Seven Golden Rules on How to Beat the Market—
Again and Again and Again 67
YALE HIRSCH, *Editor, Stock Trader's Almanac*

A Not-So-Random Walk to Stock Market Profits 69
EUGENE D. BRODY, *Senior Vice President and Director of Option Management, Oppenheimer Capital Corp.*

Invest With Your Head—Not With the Herd 73
JAMES BALOG, *Senior Executive Vice President, Drexel Burnham Lambert Inc.*

Financial Deregulation and Its Impact on Deflationary Economic
Growth and Profits in the Stock and Bond Markets 75
ARNOLD X. MOSKOWITZ, *Senior Vice President and Economist, Dean Witter Reynolds, Inc.*

Ehrlich's Cardinal Rules of Investing 83
HAROLD B. EHRLICH, *Chairman Emeritus, Bernstein-Macaulay, Inc.*

The Federal Reserve Plays the Music—and All the
Financial Markets Dance to Its Tune 85
DAVID M. JONES, *Senior Vice President and Economist, Aubrey G. Lanston & Co., Inc.*

Finding Profits in Troubled Situations   89
MONTE J. GORDON, *Vice President and Director of Research,*
   Dreyfus Corporation

Cashing In on Unexpected Developments   91
MICHAEL J. JOHNSTON, *President, Paine Webber Capital Markets Group, Inc.*

Minimizing Downside Risk by Allocating the Asset Mix   93
MARTIN D. SASS, *President, M.D. Sass Investors Services, Inc.*

The Topsy-Turvey World of Investing: Conservatism
   Versus Speculation   95
PIERRE A. RINFRET, *President, Rinfret Associates, Inc.*

Analyzing Management's Long-Term Potential   101
WILLIAM R. HAMBRECHT, *Senior Partner, Hambrecht & Quist*

If You Wouldn't Want to Own the Business, Don't Buy
   the Stock   103
LUCIEN O. HOOPER, *Vice President, Thomson McKinnon Securities, Inc.*

Concentration, Patience, and Consistency   105
ROBERT B. MENSCHEL, *Partner, Goldman, Sachs & Co.*

Don't Be Afraid to Take a Loss   107
GEORGE S. JOHNSTON, *President, Scudder, Stevens & Clark*

Cutting Losses and Letting Profits Ride   109
BERNARD J. LASKER, *Senior Partner, Lasker, Stone & Stern*

How Swiss Bankers Invest Internationally   111
HANS J. BAER, *Chairman, The Julius Baer Group, Zurich*

Ten Rules for Stock Market Failure (Or, How to
   Lose Money Without Really Trying)   115
MARK J. APPLEMAN, *Editor, The Corporate Shareholder*

It's Money That Makes the Market Go Round   117
STEFAN ABRAMS, *Chairman, Investment Policy Committee, Oppenheimer & Co.*

PART THREE
MEETING THE INSTITUTIONAL CHALLENGE

The Institutional Secret Behind the Rise in Stock Prices   125
DONALD I. TROTT, *Director of Research, Mabon, Nugent & Co.*

Institutions Set the Trend for the Stock Market   131
JEAN M. KIRK, *Vice President, T. Rowe Price Associates*

How Individual Investors Can Outperform the Giant Institutions   139
ERIC T. MILLER, *Senior Vice President and Chief Investment Policy Officer, Donaldson, Lufkin & Jenrette, Inc.*

Principles of Investing for Big Pension Funds Can Also Apply to Small Investors   147
ARTHUR WILLIAMS III, *Vice President, Pension Fund Investments, Merrill Lynch, Inc.*

PART FOUR
STOCK MARKET SECRETS

Analyzing Yourself as an Investor   151
Deciding When to Sell   157
Making Stock Market Profits for Absolutely Wrong Reasons   161
The Thursday, 3-to-4 Syndrome   163
Trading Patterns   165
A Typical Day in the Market   167

The Week's Trading, Hour-by-Hour	169
Fridays Rise More Than Mondays	171
Daily Performance Each Year: 1952–1983	173
The Best Days of the Month	175
The Best Months of the Year	177
How the Super Bowl Forecasts the Stock Market	179
Stock Market Advice Can Have a Comic Flavor	183
Long-Lasting Nuggets of Wall Street Wisdom	185

APPENDIX
THE WISE MEN AND WOMEN OF WALL STREET— AND WHERE TO FIND THEM 193

About the Author 203

Introduction

The stock market is a great equalizer. It doesn't care whether your color is white, black, or polka-dotted; if your name is in the *Social Register* or on a police blotter; whether your ancestors came over on the Mayflower or in steerage; if you were graduated from Princeton or got no farther than P.S. 92. It does care about the color of your money and how much of it you have. The more you have, the more you can make—or lose. If you have only a little, you can build it to a lot—or lose the little you have.

If this book accomplishes anything, it will be to encourage you to do some thinking about your investments. Don't be intimidated by the jargon and the seeming complexity of the market. You don't have to be the world's greatest expert to be a successful investor. What you do need to know are your own strengths and weaknesses and the extent to which you want to be involved in seeking out investment opportunities and making investment decisions.

Some people just aren't willing to spend much time at this. That's okay, providing they do spend some time to find the right person or organization to handle their investments and make sure that their objectives are understood and pursued. But even these types of investors owe it to themselves to be reasonably well informed about the game their hard-earned dollars are playing in. I hope this book will help fill that bill.

Those who want to get more involved themselves—or already are involved—should know that there's a lot they can accomplish without vast expenditures of time and effort. When all the double-talk is eliminated, it comes down to two basic elements—*what* to buy (and sell) and *when* to do it. Make those two decisions properly and you're a winner. Make them foolishly and you're a loser.

If you want to make an overnight killing in the stock market without any real risk or even serious thought, put down this book immediately. It's not for you. I'm not a stock market seer or prophet. I do not have a magic system. And I've learned to beware of investment writers who say they have such systems, or who get carried away by the size of their own egos, or who must find a new stock to recommend every week or two. Some of the best experts I know are happy to come up with an ideal stock purchase two or three times a year.

What I do have is a storehouse of common sense information and advice, gathered in more than 25 years as a journalist, most of it as a financial reporter and editor. I've rubbed shoulders with and asked pointed questions of some of Wall Street's wisest people and some of its greatest charlatans. Some have made fortunes in the stock market; others have lost fortunes. Some have done both.

Many experts swear by the patterns that appear on their intricately plotted charts. Others stake their reputations and incomes on what they glean from computer printouts. Still others are guided by what they see on the ticker tape, which, in this modern age, flashes before them magnified a hundred times on giant screens or blinks on and off from tiny display consoles sitting on their desks. "The tape never lies," they never tire of repeating. And many times they're right.

Since the dismal days of late 1974 when the Dow Jones Industrial Average plummeted to 577.60, a whole new generation of investors has come into the market. Over the following ten years, they saw the Dow edge back up over 1000 in the spring of 1981, fall to 776.92 in the summer of 1982, and then blast off to a record high of 1287.20 in November 1983. Another big rally in early 1985 sent the Dow over the 1300 mark. Along the way, investors—new and old—enjoyed big gains and suffered big losses. Most of them could have fared better if they followed some common sense investment principles and avoided some identifiable pitfalls.

You can hear some investors at cocktail parties boasting about the "hot issues" and "penny stocks" that have proved to be bonanzas for them. (Losers, even when they're in the majority, never seem to be conspicuously vocal at those same gatherings.) But hot stocks aren't the only path to investment riches, and in these pages some of Wall Street's top professionals and I will share with you some ideas on how to get there.

A note about the format of this book. I agree with Marshall McLuhan, at least in part, when he contended that the medium is the message. And so I've tried to make this book fun to read as well as informative. Too many otherwise valuable treatises on the stock market and investing are heavy going for all but the most dedicated experts. Thus, here you'll find short chapters, charts, graphs, tables, quotations, anecdotes, and aphorisms. All of them illustrate an important concept of successful investing or make a valuable point of stock market wisdom. Many of them come from the pens or mouths of others. One of the joys of an adult lifetime spent in journalism has been the opportunity to meet and interview and learn from the experts. Here, in distilled form, is some of their expertise transmitted through what I hope is the inquiring and discerning filter of my own experience and my knowledge of who the professionals worth listening to really are.

And so, here's to the challenging game of Wall Street—the greatest financial show on earth—with all its successes and failures, wisdom and foolishness, avarice and fulfillment. On with the show.

PART ONE

INVESTING IN THE 1980s

The Rebirth of America

*We grow great by dreams.
All big men are dreamers.*
—WOODROW WILSON

When the American people swept Ronald Reagan into the White House in the election of 1980 and gave him a Republican Senate and a strong minority in the House of Representatives to help him govern, I became convinced that a landmark shift in the nation's economy was under way, one that—together with internal market forces—would result in a substantial stock market boom over a period of time. That conviction led me to write *How to Cash In on the Coming Stock Market Boom,* which was published at the end of January 1982. I wrote then that "Pent-up demand for stocks—particularly as the economy recovers from a sluggish 1981, the inflation rate falls, and the bond market rallies—will send stocks booming in 1982 and beyond. I expect to see a series of new records set by the Dow Jones Industrial Average and other leading indexes over the next few years. *Investors who do not participate will miss out on one of the great buying opportunities of the decade."*

Although I obviously felt that a bull market was coming, I confess to being surprised by the explosive power of the rally that began six-and-a-half months later, in August 1982. From its low of 776.92 on August 12, the Dow shot up past 900 by the end of that month. It cracked 1000 in October 1982, hit 1100 in February 1983, and topped 1200 in April 1983. Trading volume also soared to dizzying new heights. A great many investors made a great deal of money in that record surge. But many came in late or not at all, and others got burned when the high-flying technology stocks and the sizzling new-issue boom ran out of steam in the spring of 1983.

Although many segments of the market hit their peak during that period, the Dow set another all-time high of 1287.20 in November 1983. But it began falling in the second week of the new year, largely as a result of fears of rising interest rates and the lack of progress on reducing the huge federal budget deficit.

Despite that decline, many experienced market observers believe that the bull market will resume its powerful surge in the years ahead; some even forecast that the Dow will reach 3000 by the end of the 1980s. One top Wall Street executive, Lee H. Idleman, now research director of Neuberger & Berman, even makes the case for a 5000 Dow by the end of the century. He bases that prediction on a solid rise in corporate earnings (to a total of $400 a share for the combined 30 Dow industrial stocks) plus an increase in the Dow's price-earnings multiple to 12.5, which, while higher than it has been in recent years, is still below-average historically.

The election of Ronald Reagan in November 1980 set in motion the fundamental shift in American economic policy that underlies much—though by no means all—of the foundation for the past and future bull market of the 1980s. By sweeping into the White House a steadfast conservative who only a few years before had been considered too far right to be President, the nation signaled its demand for a change. Although most Americans supported many of the specific programs Reagan was committed to curtailing—and wanted continued government help in those aspects of their activities that benefited them individually—they were clearly in favor of less government involvement in their lives, their businesses, and especially their pocketbooks. A new sense of direction was clearly in order.

The basic problems confronting the new administration and the country had three root causes—Vietnam, Watergate, and OPEC—each of which had profoundly affected the nation's character and had shaken its self-confidence. For the first time since the Great Depression, large numbers of Americans were worrying that the financial security they had come to expect was seriously threatened. Fear of the future, rather than confidence in continued growth and prosperity, became a reality. The warnings of the doomsayers—dismissed by most people in the past—showed signs of coming true. The affluence that had previously outdistanced, or at least kept pace with, inflation was losing the race.

Vietnam had shattered the consciences of many Americans and had helped warp the perceptions of a whole generation of young people toward the time-honored values of most of their elders. When the Watergate scandal unfolded, showing a horrified nation excesses of government that were worse than even the most cynical had imagined, loss of confidence in the established order was no longer the province of the young and radical. But it was the oil crisis and the Arab embargo that proved more devastating and long-lasting than an unpopular war and political scandal.

More than anything else, the oil crisis may have led to the election of Jimmy Carter to the White House. But, in office, Carter had failed to demonstrate the sophistication and leadership ability needed to mobilize a nation beset by massive problems that steadily grew in magnitude: inflation, energy shortages, unemployment, and finally recession. Small-town verities had translated into country-bumpkin ineptitude, and the President and his attendant mediocrities were swept aside.

Tell the American people that they have to consider what's best for America and not just for themselves, and you may infuse in them a new and vibrant spirit of courage and determination. Tell them they're suffering from a national malaise, and they're likely to believe it, particularly when the disease of inflation daily strips them of their hard-earned gains.

Inflation, among its other deadly faults, robs a nation of its trust in government. As people see their buying power diminish, their savings erode, and their hopes for the future diminish, they resort to attempts to cheat the discredited governmental apparatus of what they consider its unjust due. Tax avoidance—familiar in many European countries, but, until recently, not a way of life in this country—has become widespread. The underground economy is flourishing, and getting paid "off the books" has become fashionable.

The election of Ronald Reagan reflected the determination of the American people to do something about inflation, to reduce the level of government involvement in their affairs, and to get the nation's economic machine moving again. A new spirit seemed to be sweeping America, a spirit as much psychological as ideological.

The Reagan administration's economic program received a big early impetus from the overwhelming passage of its proposed major cutbacks in federal spending. Taxes proved a more difficult task, but the White House and Congress finally hammered out individual and business tax cuts that gave the President most, though not all, of what he wanted.

After a series of false starts and stops under Carter, the Federal Reserve (the Fed), with strong sideline support from the Reagan administration, finally got across the message that it meant business in restraining the growth of the money supply, and a sustained period of extreme monetary tightening helped bring down the rate of inflation even more sharply than had been hoped for initially.

Investor euphoria over the Reagan victory and his early months in office gave the stock market a big boost, despite the largely unexpected rebound of interest rates. But, the continuation of those high levels—combined with a slowing economy and growing fears that the administration's planned defense build-up on top of the tax cuts would mean a much higher budget deficit than had been forecast—drove the market into a sharp tailspin starting in mid-1981. At the same time, the economy was falling into the worst recession since the Great Depression of the 1930s and unemployment was shooting upward. As some economists were talking about the possibility of another depression, and as the possible default of Third World nations threatened to unravel the international debt structure, the Fed loosened its grip on the monetary controls in the late spring and summer of 1982 and interest rates began a dramatic decline. Bond prices zoomed and the stock market started the greatest bull market in its history.

Despite such serious economic problems as the massive acceleration of the federal budget deficit and the continuation of high interest rates (even as inflation dropped sharply, *real* interest rates—meaning after adjusting for inflation—remained at record levels), the stock market as a whole confounded predictions by some gloom-and-doomers that another sharp drop was in the offing and retained most of its 1982–1983 gains. But there were some disturbing developments as the nation moved into another fateful Presidential election year. After an explosive first week, when the Dow industrials came within a whisker of another record high, the market began to drift down as the White House and Congress failed to act on cutting the budget deficit. At the same time, the economy recorded two quarters of unsustainably high growth, leading the Federal Reserve to clamp down on the money supply once again in an effort to head off a resurgence of inflation. Interest rates rose and the stock market slumped, hitting its 1984 low of 1086.57 on the Dow in July. From there, apparently anticipating another Reagan election victory in November and spurred by an easier Fed monetary policy and falling interest rates, the market staged a sharp rally, including a record day of volume on the New York Stock Exchange, when 236.6 million shares changed hands. From there, the Dow trended downward, with the exception of a pre-election rally and a short burst in December that carried the Dow to 1211.57 by year's end.

But short-term moves aside, there are a number of fundamental reasons to expect the market to move sharply upward during the second half of the 1980s:

1. Demographics will have an increasingly significant impact on the market in the years ahead. The post-World War II baby boom, lasting from 1947 through 1964, produced an average of 4.4 million births a year. The offspring of that population explosion constitutes nearly a third of the nation's total population. The older members of that group are now in their thirties and late twenties, just the age level when they are feeling their financial oats and beginning to turn their thoughts from consumption to investment. Career patterns are becoming established, earnings potentials are substantial, and self-confidence is high. As the stock market picks up momentum and investing contagion spreads, this age group will contribute a new pool of investors ready and eager to join the game, thus adding more fuel to the demand for equities.

2. The demand for stocks by big financial institutions will continue to grow at a tremendous rate, particularly to fill the skyrocketing needs of the pension funds they manage. The U.S. Department of Labor forecasts that the annual contribution to pension funds will rise from $32 billion in 1975 to $72 billion in 1985 and $137 billion in 1995. The earnings of such funds will increase from $16 billion in 1975 to $269 billion in 1995, by which time the total pool of pension fund assets will reach $2.9 trillion. Since the total market value of all American equities is now well under half that figure, the implications of that growth for the stock market is enormous.

3. Whipsawed by the bond market debacles of recent years, institutional money managers will move out of bonds and into stocks, changing the asset mix of the funds they manage. This will be a slow process, but it will have profound implications for the stock market, considering the tremendous size of the sums involved.

4. The deregulation moves set in motion by the Carter administration and accelerated under President Reagan will serve to reduce government interference with business and eliminate some of the attendant costs. Although it has become too simple to lump all regulation together as counterproductive and to overlook the tremendous social and business benefits it has provided, it's clear, too, that regulation has restrained productivity and siphoned off funds that would have gone into other forms of investment. Perhaps most restrictive, however, has been the uncertainty engendered by the vagueness and changeability of federal regulations. Businesses, like markets, abhor uncertainty, and the unpredictable nature of some regulations has made the situation even worse. The Reagan administration's tougher stance on regulation removed more of the unnecessary shackles and allows the free market greater latitude in which to operate.

5. *The valuation of common stocks will be ready for a dramatic move upward.* In the period following World War II, as the nation turned its military-based technology and productive capacity to the consumer sector, price/earnings (P/E) ratios were dramatically revalued—from 7 in the late 1940s to 15–20 in the late 1950s. They remained fairly constant during the period of relative stability that lasted from 1958 to 1972. But then, as energy prices exploded, inflation increased, productivity lagged, and the dollar slumped. P/E ratios began falling back to the levels that existed just after World War II. P/E levels, for many of the reasons mentioned previously in this chapter, can be expected to be revalued upward, with a resulting profound effect on stock prices.

How to Remove the Stress from Investing

All men that are ruined are ruined on the side of their natural propensities.
—EDMUND BURKE

Richard Russell, the respected publisher of the *Dow Theory Letters* (La Jolla, California), notes that some people feel guilty about having made or inherited large amounts of money and therefore subconsciously try to get rid of their money by stupid investments or excessive trading. Others unconsciously put themselves in stressful investing situations, perhaps to take their minds off their real problems. Nonetheless, he says, every investment and speculation imposes a toll on the psyche of the investor. Over a period of thirty-five years of handling his own money, Russell has developed the following seven rules on how to relieve the stress of investing:

1. Never lose sight of the idea that you are investing to make money. That sounds simple, but it isn't. The corollary: Don't invest for thrills. If you do, the odds are that you'll get a lot more thrills than you bargained for.

2. Does the investment make sense from a risk/reward standpoint, taxes considered? Remember, it takes a real pro to skip a situation in which he is reasonably sure that the item is going higher in price, yet the risk/reward still may not warrant his taking a position.

3. Remember that the market is always there. There's nothing wrong with missing a move. There is everything wrong with overtrading and overinvesting. Often it is worthwhile sitting on the sidelines just to catch your breath—or to gain perspective. Remember the old market adage, "When in doubt—stay out!"

4. Stay off margin. Margin is the guaranteed road to stress. I'm not saying that margin users don't make money. I'm saying that margin users invite stress. A short-seller borrows stock and then sells that stock short. To that extent he is margined. For 90 percent of investors, I say, avoid the short side of the market. A few pros know how to make money on the short side, but most people lose money in shorts. Despite what you might hear to the contrary, shorting requires an entirely different psychology than going long. Forget shorting!

5. Always keep in mind the "magic" of compound interest. Making a fortune with the help of compound interest requires only three things: the ability to save, patience, and time. Most people have all three, but they are unaware that they do.

6. When you make a mistake, admit it to yourself—then act. The two catastrophic procedures in investing are to stay wrong and to compound a mistake, for instance to average down on a stock that is sliding to new lows.

7. Most important, don't waste time worrying about things that you can't do anything about or that you have no intention of doing anything about.

The People Quotient

It ain't so much the things we don't know that get us into trouble. It's the things we know that ain't so.
—ARTEMUS WARD

In 1964, I was called back from Europe, where I was serving as a foreign correspondent for the *New York Herald Tribune*, covering Germany and the European Common Market, to be the paper's financial editor. In those halcyon, though final, days of one of America's greatest newspapers, the *Trib* engaged in a good deal of self-promotion (there was ample room for "house ads" since our pages weren't exactly brimming over with paid advertising). And so the promotion department sent a fellow to interview me for the preparation of such an ad. I had never met him before, and alas, I can't recall his name. We spent an hour together and he plied me with piercing questions about my philosophy of covering business news and my plans for the paper's financial pages. Then the ad on me appeared, running a full two columns of the paper. The headline said, *Myron Kandel thinks people are more important than money . . . that's why he's financial editor of the New York Herald Tribune.* I was really struck by how accurate a description of my thinking that was, even though I had never articulated it in that way. And although friends and colleagues have needled me about that slogan, the years have only confirmed my belief that people are indeed more important than money when it comes to understanding how the world of business and finance really operates.

That's especially true of the stock market. Our thinking is often colored by what we see in print about the market. After all, the daily papers are filled with full pages of stock and bond quotations, and most financial news stories concentrate on dollar signs rather than people. But the canny investor must keep his eye on the people as well as the figures. The most-admired investor/speculator/financier/elder statesman of this century, Bernard Baruch, put it simply: "The stock market is people." He was talking primarily about that collective group of investors whose day-by-day (and even minute-by-minute) decisions determine whether any specific stock—and the market as a whole—goes up or down. Psychology, which Webster defines as the science of human behavior, is a great determinant of market behavior.

But there is another crucial "people" element in picking stocks. That involves the people who run the companies whose stocks we choose to buy or sell. Good management usually means good companies. Successful investors follow this principle, which has been around a long time. Malcolm Forbes, the owner of *Forbes,* whose father edited the magazine before him, recalls: "My father used to say that he never bought the stock of a company based on its balance sheet. He always bought management, based on his personal impression of the top man, the guy at the steering wheel. . . . If they're capable and have the qualities that fit the company and the era and the industry's needs at the moment, that's of far greater value to a potential investor than whatever reserves the company may have or how long it's been in business."

And then Malcolm Forbes added, "It's easy to forget that the benefit or harm of decisions made today in corporations, particularly large corporations, may not be reaped for four or five years, so what you'd better know is the caliber of the men making the decisions now. Those are enormous chips they're playing with, and if they don't have the ability to make the right decisions now, the company is going to eventually get into trouble."

And Mark J. Appleman, an author-turned-stockbroker-turned-management consultant, points out succinctly: "Some people bet on the jockey as well as the horse."

How to Identify Companies That Will Turn Into Winners

It's more important to be right about stocks than right about the stock market.
—SIDNEY B. LURIE

I'm always amused, and annoyed as well, when the press describes an actor, singer, or musician as an overnight success. Usually, long years of training and working in obscurity have prepared the way for that sudden acclaim. The same is often true of companies that suddenly grab the investment limelight. The groundwork has been laid long before. It's during those years that astute investors can make the biggest gains. How can such companies be identified?

The Wall Street house of Drexel Burnham Lambert long known for its solid fundamental research into companies of all sizes, has developed these four key criteria for evaluating a company's potential for significant success.

1. Management. Tomorrow's performance will largely be a reflection of today's management decisions. That's why the caliber of management is the single most critical factor in corporate success.

2. Productivity. Profits must be preceded by sales, and sales must be preceded by a minimum level of cost benefit. The company must offer either comparable products at a lower cost or demonstrably superior products at a competitive cost. Companies with the highest productivity levels inevitably compete better because they can offer superior value. Most often, productivity is linked to companies that are market leaders or that dominate a specialized niche of a given market.

3. Innovation. The key here is linking innovation with reality. It's a matter of relating innovative technology to real world markets and marketing opportunities.

4. Capital strength. Many valuable ideas fail to succeed for lack of adequate financing. It takes capital to turn ideas into reality, to develop new technology, to translate technologies into products or services, to take products or services to market, and to stay on the course even in the face of setbacks along the way.

You Can Make Your Own Investment Discoveries

First I look for a need in the society, then I look for the industries that are going to fill that need and then for the companies that will fill that need most profitably.
—CARL HATHAWAY

When miniskirts were just becoming the vogue, the wife of a young Wall Street analyst came home one day enthusiastic over the pantyhose she had bought at a reasonable price. Pantyhose, of course, eliminated the risk that short skirts would expose the band at the top of conventional nylon stockings. In the midst of his wife's enthusiasm over the advantages of the pantyhose, the analyst realized that they also would require much more of the texturized fabric than the amount used on regular hose. He began looking into the impact of growing demand for such fabric on the few companies that made it. As a result, he recommended buying those stocks well before they became a hot fad on Wall Street.

Can an average investor unschooled in securities analysis and lacking the time and resources of the professional analyst do the same? Not in such detail, but he can develop enough material on the subject to come to the realization that here is a group of stocks ripe for some rapid growth.

A Manhattan market analyst noticed more and more people—men as well as women—wearing sneakers and other comfortable shoes while traveling to work and then changing into more suitable office attire. He investigated the leading makers of such footwear and made big profits on two of them once the rest of the market recognized their improved performance.

First-hand observations can also work the other way. A very successful broker I know worked for one of the country's biggest investment houses in his early days. When one of his active customers, a middle-aged woman, came to him for some investment ideas, he told her about a lengthy report he had just received from the home office extolling the virtues of a retailing company. She listened politely as he recounted the company's financial leverage and other esoteric details, and then excused herself. She came back an hour later, having visited one of the company's near-by outlets. "Don't buy the stock," she advised him. "There's nobody in the store." The chain went bankrupt not long afterward.

Sometimes the handwriting is on the wall, but we're too busy to look up and discover that it's there. Take the fellow in Vermont who got worried early in the OPEC game about all the talk of a potential heating oil shortage. So he decided to go out and buy a wood stove, only to find they were all sold out. A lot of other people had decided to do the same thing. So this enterprising fellow/entrepreneur ended up by setting up his own woodstove manufacturing and distribution company. He made a bundle.

We all can't go off and start a business every time we perceive a good business opportunity. But we can seek out those existing companies that stand to benefit from the opportunity we've uncovered. And buy a piece of them—even if it's just a hundred shares.

Sticking close to home can offer many opportunities for investment success. Canny doctors have long profited from their knowledge of how a pharmaceutical or medical supply company is doing. Is a promising new drug coming on the market? Might it make a substantial impact in its field, as well as on its maker's sales picture? Conversely, does a highly touted new product have potential problems?

Is a company shaping up smartly, or is it lagging? Whatever your business or profession, and whatever your level of expertise, you will be surprised how many such observations you can make on your own. Use them—in conjunction with more stock market-directed factors—to help you make your investment decisions. Common sense can be a lot more profitable than supposedly inside tips, although the latter may get a lot more cocktail party attention.

Be Ready to Seize Sudden Opportunities

Bull markets are born during periods of mass pessimism.
—RALPH A. ROTNEM

Keep an eye out for unexpected investment opportunities. For example, take the case of Consolidated Edison Co. of New York (Con Ed), which ran into a cash squeeze back in 1974 and had to pass its dividend. Long considered a safe investment, even for those proverbial widows and orphans, Con Ed's move threw consternation into the bond market. Not only did its bonds take a tumble, but those of other utilities also fell, as did the bonds of similarly rated companies in totally different fields. The result, in Con Ed's case, was that the bonds, which were selling at close to par (or $100) before the company's directors voted to omit the dividend on April 23, 1974, plunged to $54 by the end of August. A canny investor willing to take some risks but feeling that there was no way the utility serving New York City was going to fail could have made big profits when the price climbed back to $80 by the following June. Even more significant was the effect of the Con Ed move on totally unrelated companies. For example, the interest rate spread between AAA-rated corporate bonds and AA utilities widened from 87 basis points to 136 basis points in a few months. (Note: In bond market parlance, 100 basis points equals one percentage point.) The risk premium fell by 75 basis points between July and November 1974. But before long, after investors had time to think about what happened, the risk premium began to fall. As a result, investors who bought AA utilities profited even more than those who played it safer with AAA corporates.

Moral: The market often will overreact to a dire event, at least for a short period of time. Such events make for unusually attractive buying opportunities. If you recognize the situation but don't feel confident enough to make the specific selections yourself, find a broker who understands the game—or has the expertise in his firm to do so—and begin cashing in.

Pick a Good Stock and Never Let It Go

*Money doesn't make you happy,
but it quiets the nerves.*
—SEAN O'CASEY

When Michael Robbins, now one of the canniest floor members of the New York Stock Exchange, was a young stockbroker in the early 1960s, he became fascinated with the potential of Dow Jones & Co., which published the *Wall Street Journal, Barron's Weekly,* and the *Dow Jones News Service.* His reasoning was that the company had a virtually exclusive franchise on essential sources of information for the business community —particularly in the daily newspaper—and thus had great growth potential.

The trouble was that Dow Jones stock, held mostly by members of the founding families and by executives of the company and its publications, was rarely traded. Robbins visited William Kerby, then a Dow Jones vice president who later was to become its chief executive officer, in search of some stock. Kerby suggested that he try a small bank in Florida, which handled the trusts of some retired Dow Jones people. The trust officer there said he did have 100 shares available for sale, and so the enterprising young broker bought all of them and apportioned them among some of his clients at $650 a share.

Twenty years later, in mid-February 1981, Robbins received the following note from one of them, a retired New York City bank official: "You may have forgotten that back in 1961, you made it possible for me to buy one share of Dow Jones & Co. Inc., which I gave to my wife as a Valentine, and the certificate was dated February 14, 1961. That one share through splits is now 90 shares, and later this spring will be 180 shares. . . . While I said 'thank you' in 1961, I am writing to say it again. We are both grateful."

At the time of the letter, Dow Jones stock was selling at $62 per share, making the 90 shares worth $5,580 (in addition to all the dividends paid in the meantime). On February 14, 1984, the stock closed at 40⅞ making the by-now 360 shares worth more than $7,000. Not bad for a $650 investment.

Watch Out for Those Get-Rich-Quick Schemes

If you sit in on a poker game and you don't see a sucker at the table, get up. Because you're the sucker.
—JOHN SPOONER

Don't be misled by "how-to-get-rich-quick" schemes. If you really want to throw the dice, why pick the stock market? Go to Las Vegas or Atlantic City, put down $100 worth of chips on the craps table when it's your turn to handle the dice, and if you throw fourteen winners in a row, walk away with a cool $1.6 million. It could be that easy. Of course, the two-letter word "if" means a lot. The odds against winning fourteen times in a row are astronomical.

You can gamble in the stock market, too. The results aren't as suddenly apparent as they are at the gaming tables, and you're unlikely to lose your whole wad on one throw. But losing can hurt even more when it happens in slow stages.

You can play the market to make a big killing. You can also invest for sounder reasons: to supplement your income, to hedge against inflation, to build up funds for retirement, or for a specific goal like buying a home or putting your kids through college. Depending upon your individual circumstances, you can be aggressive in pursuing such objectives—but you don't have to stack the odds against yourself to make money in the stock market.

The alacrity with which normally intelligent individuals jump at the thought of getting a hot tip is astounding. No matter that it comes from a source that's proven unreliable in the past or from someone with unknown credentials. Some investors seem to insist on getting burned. Bernard Baruch observed, "When beggars and shoeshine boys, barbers and beauticians tell you how to get rich, it is time to remind yourself that there is no more dangerous illusion than the belief that one can get something for nothing."

The story is told in Wall Street about the renowned stock promoter who, when he was ready to unload a stock he had helped push up, would drop a scrap of paper, apparently by accident, in a theater or restaurant. On the paper was scrawled the words: *Buy XYZ Company.* Finders of the paper, knowing the promoter's reputation, would hurry to tell their friends. As the word got around the next morning, the canny promoter would be able to sell his shares in a rising market.

When to Sit With a Stock —And When to Keep Moving

Don't try to buy at the bottom and sell at the top. This can't be done, except by liars.
—BERNARD BARUCH

Why not just pick out a stock with a good growth potential and sit with it? That's a question frequently asked by those investors who prefer to buy and then hold through thick and thin. And as a prime example of how thick it can get, they point to Xerox. Back in 1956, when the company was still named Haloid Co. and had only just bought the patent rights to the xerographic process, Xerox was selling at an adjusted price of $3 a share. *Fortune* magazine took a look at the stock's performance ten years later and found that in mid-1966 the tremendous success of its photocopying business had skyrocketed Xerox stock to $245.75, an astonishing gain of 8,092 percent. An investment of less than $13,000 in Haloid stock would have mushroomed to $1 million in just one decade.

That performance is obviously a great reason for buying the right stock and putting it away. (In fairness, however, it should be pointed out that if an investor had sold the stock at its high point and bought it back at its subsequent low point during each of those years—as if such timing were possible!—the value of the shares owned by mid-1966 would have been into the *billions*.) But that's getting away from my point, which is that while owning and holding Haloid/Xerox during that ten-year period would have been a masterstroke of investing genius, doing the same thing for the next ten years would have resulted in a gain of only (!) a little better than 500 percent. That's nothing to sneeze at, but it's a long way from the better than 8,000 percent profit of the earlier period.

All of which means holding—as well as buying and selling—can be a crucial determinant to stock market success.

Winning with the Losers —and Vice Versa

It is an ill wind that blows nobody good.
—OLD ENGLISH PROVERB

When I was sports editor of the campus newspaper at Brooklyn College, an institution of superior learning in the heart of Flatbush noted more for its subway scholars than for its bruising linemen, we were fond of proving how our football team mathematically defeated Notre Dame each season (e.g., we lost by only 7 points to N.Y.U., which trounced Susquehanna by 32, which lost to Pittsburgh by 12, which defeated Notre Dame by 14.)

Similarly, you can make yourself a huge winner or loser—on paper—by twisting statistics. Nevertheless, figures can tell a lot about stock market performance. No matter how bad a beating a stock takes, it has a high and a low for the year. Does this sound like another of those stock market truisms? Think again. Take the ten biggest winners of 1984 on the New York Stock Exchange and examine when their highs and lows occurred. Do the same for the ten biggest losers. Despite the trend for the year, you can see that there usually was big money to be made in the losers and big money to be lost in the winners.

Squeezing the Dollar

It's OK to be wrong, but it's criminal to stay wrong.
—RICHARD RUSSELL

When I was the *Herald Tribune*'s correspondent for Germany in the early 1960s, my friend Antony Terry, who covered much of Central and Eastern Europe for the *Sunday Times* of London, confided to me once that he always carried $1,000 in American money when he traveled. The reason: No matter where he was—particularly in Communist countries short of hard currency—U.S. greenbacks would be instantly accepted. That cash, he said, had come in very handy in chartering airplanes for a sudden dash to an out-of-the-way place or for other activities about which he preferred not to go into detail. After all, he reminded me, the American dollar was as good as gold.

Well, for a while that wasn't true, and the dollar fell into the international monetary doghouse. During that period, I suspect that the Tony Terrys of the world were carrying around gold pieces for the same purpose. But after gold hit its all-time high above $850 an ounce in early 1981 and then began falling, and the dollar started to regain its strength, American greenbacks again became the world's premier currency.

What do the fluctuations of the dollar mean for the investor? First, they mean that if you're interested in buying foreign stocks, you must evaluate the strength of that country's currency as well as the merits of the specific companies you're interested in. It gains you nothing to buy a stock that appreciates 25 percent in price if the currency involved drops by a similar amount. Similarly, if both the stock and the currency fall, you suffer a double loss. On the other hand, you can double your gain if the stock and the currency go up. There's leverage both ways.

In addition, a strong dollar makes U.S. exports more expensive abroad, and so a company heavily dependent on selling its products overseas might feel an impact on its sales. Conversely, if a company buys much of its raw materials or components overseas, and pays for them in a depreciated foreign currency, its costs would be lower. At the same time, foreign items imported into this country would cost less and thus be more competitive with domestic products.

So keep in mind that the status of the dollar on the foreign exchange markets can indeed influence the price at which both domestic and foreign stocks will be selling.

Picking the Right Stockbroker

There is grief in indecision.
—CICERO

Yale Hirsch, author and investment letter writer, contends that before choosing a stockbroker an investor must understand his or her own investment personality. "One of the major reasons investors 'chew up' brokers," he says, "is because the investor often does not know what he or she really wants. When the investor does not know, it is utterly impossible for the broker to know. Many investors are not honest with themselves, and this fact causes no end of problems between the investor and his or her broker."

At the same time, Hirsch notes in his *Directory of Exceptional Brokers* (The Hirsch Organization, 1982), that "It's masochistic to deal with a broker who doesn't have a rapport with you." Investors should enjoy their relationship with their brokers and refuse to be pushed around, he says. Hirsch adds 'The broker-investor relationship doesn't have to be a cocktail party, but it shouldn't be a guerrilla war of conflicting personalities, either." He also recommends that serious investors who use a variety of investment strategies should employ the services of more than one broker, dealing with those who specialize in those strategies.

Claude N. Rosenberg, Jr., a highly regarded San Francisco securities analyst, market letter writer, and author for many years before starting a successful money management firm (Rosenberg Capital Management), offers these eight succinct tips on the characteristics an investor should look for in selecting the right stockbroker:

1. Obvious honesty and integrity; the client's interest should always come first.

2. An in-depth knowledge of the business.

3. A person who understands risks and who can give you a good idea of the risk you are taking in anything you buy.

4. Sufficient imagination to produce better-than-average results.

5. Strong personal discipline that shapes his (or her) approach to the market and stock selection.

6. Someone who recognizes the importance of structuring your investments to achieve realistic goals.

7. A person whose investment personality complements your own.

8. Someone who comprehends the psychological aspects of investing as they relate to you, to himself or herself, and to the market as a whole.

How to Unlock the Secrets of the Annual Report

A cynic is one who, smelling flowers, looks for a coffin.
—H.L. MENCKEN

If you know how to use it, the corporate annual report can be a highly revealing document. Huge amounts of corporate cash and executive time go into its preparation and distribution. All too often, however, investors pay hardly any attention to the annual report, since some of the profit and loss information it contains has been released earlier. Also, it's not exactly light reading. That's too bad, because the report is also crammed full of information that can have an important bearing on the market value of a security. This information may be spelled out in flowing detail in the chief executive's letter or hidden in a terse footnote. Investors who overlook the annual reports of companies whose stock they own or are thinking of buying do so at their own peril. One of the best short guides I've seen on how to read an annual report has been prepared by Stanley Lanzet, a securities analyst at Drexel Burnham Lambert Inc., which includes the following advice:

What to look for?

Potential capital gains and/or current income are the chief reasons behind most investments. Therefore, in scrutinizing an annual report, investors are seeking to identify the factors that underlie past operating trends and those that are likely to provide for future growth. The checklist of items to look for might include:

1. The forthrightness of management in evaluating the past successes achieved and the disappointments sustained by the company. Are the shortfalls being constantly attributed to external events (for instance, a strike at a supplier's plant, the soaring cost of some important raw material, high interest rates and hard economic times)? Are the good years chiefly attributed to the managerial prowess of company officials? We emphasize that managements often unfairly receive the credit for results that were caused by events largely outside of their control. Good management allows companies to literally be masters of their own fate.

2. The objectives being set for future earnings growth and return on investment. Often an indication is provided in the chief executive's letter as to the prognosis for the current year's profits. For illustrative purposes, we will be referring to the fiscal 1983 (ended September 30) annual report of the Black & Decker Manufacturing Company.

In the fiscal 1983 annual, Black & Decker management indicated that "a marked improvement in profitability for fiscal 1984" was expected. This is based on "the forecasts for a good economy in the United States, and a modest economic recovery in Western Europe." Black & Decker also took a number of vigorous steps to boost profitability, including the sale of the deficit-plagued McCulloch gasoline chain saw and the medical power tool product divisions; the lowering of manufacturing overhead by the closing of three plants; and the cutting of management and marketing overhead costs via the elimination of a layer of corporate management and the reduction of the size of operations in "third world" countries where harsh economic conditions were generating losses. Management also discusses some continuing problems, namely the strong dollar (negative translation effect); the persistence of difficult economic conditions in some parts of the world (especially France and Italy); and the intense competitive climate in the professional power tool market.

3. The steps being taken to achieve these goals—plans for new products, marketing programs and capital additions.

In the past, Black & Decker has based its growth targets on the strong underlying need for its products (portable electric tools), the escalation in labor costs, "especially in services for the home, increases in leisure time, and the need for self-achievement in increasingly complex societies that provide less and less opportunity for individual accomplishments." Other avenues of expansion include the broadening of the product line. For example, the company has developed new kinds of power tools such as an electric power planer and a hot air paint stripper. Recent product introductions include staplers, planers, heat guns, bench tools, sanders, car care products, and home cleaning and lighting products. Black & Decker is seeking to reduce costs and to become more efficient and productive.

4. The prospects for realizing these goals: How rapidly are the company's markets expanding? Will the company have to widen its share of the market to achieve its growth target? How does the company compete (price or quality)? What would be the likely response of the company's competitors to a loss of market share?

Black & Decker has usually focused its efforts on labor-saving products that have above-average growth potential. It has established a broad distribution network that provides access to more than 100,000 retail outlets throughout the world. The company has constantly sought to be first in new product introductions in its sector (for example, the world's first cordless drill and first cordless hedge trimmer) and has also striven to improve the performance and quality of its products. The brand name is well respected and management has been able, on a long-term basis, to effectively respond to changes in market conditions. In the major world consumer markets, the company has, on average, over a 50 percent share of the market. Over long periods of time, year-to-year earnings declines have been unusual events for Black & Decker. Perhaps, the decision to get out of a mature market, gasoline chain saws, signals the intention of management to emphasize the basic strengths of the company. The future of Black & Decker resides in the development of new products, in our view.

5. The changing character of the enterprise: Is the company maturing? Is the cyclicality of the business increasing or decreasing? Are the once-proprietary products of the company turning into commodity-type items?

Turning back once again to Black & Decker, the company is unlikely to repeat the dramatic two-to-three year surges in earnings that it enjoyed when it was a much smaller entity, as the sales base has expanded about three-fold in the past decade to $1,168 million in fiscal 1983. The cyclicality of the earnings stream has grown decidedly more pronounced. Black & Decker posted its first down year in the last sixteen in fiscal 1975 when it proved vulnerable to the severe recession prevailing during that time period. Furthermore, Black & Decker's earnings from continuing operations have declined in each of the last four fiscal years. We note that the company's past innovations have resulted in the spawning of competition and that Black & Decker has kept its edge through constantly improving the product line. Management notes the need "to return to acceptable levels of earnings" and "to reduce our vulnerability to economic volatility."

6. The capital needs of the company: Will the internal cash flow be sufficient to provide for both the growth objectives and a higher level of cash dividends? Will the payout ratio widen or contract?

Black & Decker has the means of internally financing many of its growth objectives. The company's cash position was $158 million at the close of fiscal 1983. The balance sheet was bolstered by an $85 million equity offering and the introduction of aggressive working capital management programs.

7. The structure of the management team: Is this essentially a one-man show, or a broad-based management effort?

In our view, Black & Decker has successfully made the transition to a large and diverse business enterprise and has adequate depth of management.

8. The likely trend in earnings: Is the growth rate slowing or accelerating? Were there any unusual causes behind a sudden one-year spurt or plunge in earning power?

Black & Decker's earnings have deteriorated drastically in the last four years. Prior to fiscal 1980, net income had increased at approximately a 15 percent pace for the preceding twenty years. The one down year during that period was attributed to a marked slowing in sales growth—up just 2 percent—in fiscal 1975 due to the surplus inventory position of its products at the retail level. Black & Decker's performance in the last several years has been adversely affected by the recession that has gripped the economies of most major industrialized nations. Black & Decker, in our judgment, has the financial resources and management skill to rebound in a more favorable economic milieu. However, it is likely that the growth rate of Black & Decker in the 1980s will be considerably lower than it enjoyed in the 1970s.

How to find it?

Probably the first item to check is the auditor's opinion to see whether or not it is a clean one—"in conformity with generally accepted accounting principles consistently applied"—or is qualified in regard to differences between the auditor and company management in the accounting treatment of some major item, or in the outcome of important litigation. Largely due to the growing incidence of shareholder suits in recent years, auditors have begun issuing more and more qualified opinions. In essence, the auditor's opinion provides a good indication of the reliability of the company's financial statements. Black & Decker has a clean opinion from its auditors.

The footnotes should be read next. Special attention should be paid to year-to-year changes in foreign-currency translations, extraordinary items (for example, a capital gain on the sale of a plant, or a special credit from the settlement of a lawsuit), the effective tax rate, the percentage changes in the allowance for doubtful accounts, and research and development expenditures. Sometimes a careful reading of the footnotes can indicate whether an outstanding earnings increase was the result of an astute accountant's pencil. The chief executive's letter and the other descriptive material should then be perused. By itself, the exercise doesn't mean much, but a great deal can be ascertained if it is done in conjunction with the examination of the statements made by management in previous annual reports.

An Information Checklist

Annual reports usually contain the following data:

- A company description. In essence, what the enterprise's operations consist of and a general outline of how the company conducts its business.

- A table showing the company's relevant financial data for at least the past five years. Included in the presentation would be sales, earnings before taxes, net income, earnings per share and the dividend. Many companies will also list such important ratios as rate of return on shareholders' equity, current ratio, pretax and after-tax profit margins and dividend payout ratio.

- An analysis of the income statement for at least several years. In short, what factors accounted for the increase or decrease in net income.

- Complete income statements and balance sheets and cash flow statements for the past two years.

- A summary of the accounting policies used by the company.

- A breakdown of the company's sales, net income and identifiable assets by business segment and geographic area.

- A quarterly breakdown of sales and earnings for the last two years.

- A list of the company's directors and officers.

The Relevant Ratios

THOSE MEASURING LIQUIDITY

1. The Current Ratio

$$\frac{\text{Current Assets}}{\text{Current Liabilities}} = \frac{\$662.5}{\$238.7} = 2.8:1$$

2. The Quick Asset Ratio

$$\frac{\text{Cash, marketable securities, receivables}}{\text{Current Liabilities}} = \frac{\$147.1 + \$10.8 + \$260.4}{\$238.7} = 1.8:1$$

This test of a company's ability to pay its current obligations is far more stringent than the current ratio, as it concentrates on those assets which have a high degree of liquidity and which have a reasonably known valuation.

THOSE MEASURING DEBT

1. Total Debt to Total Assets

$$\frac{\text{Total debt}[1]}{\text{Total assets}} = \frac{\$20.4 + \$159.1}{985.4} = 18.2\%$$

[1] Both short- and long-term.

2. Long-Term Debt to Shareholders' Equity

$$\frac{\text{Long-Term Debt}}{\text{Shareholders' Equity}} = \frac{\$159.1}{\$554.4} = 28.7\%$$

These ratios should prove useful in evaluating a company's ability to meet its short-term and long-term obligations during difficult times.

THOSE MEASURING PROFITABILITY

1. Return on Average Shareholders' Equity

$$\frac{\text{Net Income}[1]}{\text{Shareholders' Equity}[2]} = \frac{\$28.2}{\$502.4} = 5.6\%$$

[1] From continuing operations.
[2] The average of shareholders' equity at the beginning and end of the year.

This ratio measures the return received by the owners of the business after all income taxes and interest expenses have been paid.

2. Profit Margin

$$\frac{\text{Earnings before interest and taxes}}{\text{Sales}} = \frac{\$91.8}{\$1,167.8} = 7.9\%$$

This ratio aids in the evaluation of a company's efficiency, when appraised in relation to other companies in its industry.

NOTE: All of the numbers contained in the above examples are in millions of dollars and are from Black & Decker's fiscal 1983 income statement or balance sheet.

Filling in the Gaps

Astute investors realize the huge gulfs in information that remain to be filled in order to properly analyze most non-regulated publicly held companies, despite the enormous quantity of material available—for example, annual and quarterly earnings reports, prospectuses, press releases on important corporate developments, brochures on major products, presentations before analyst groups, brokerage house reports and analyses from such financial services as Standard & Poor's, Moody's and ValueLine.

Another facet of the time-consuming task of gathering information is developing a profile of the industries in which the company participates. This can be accomplished by reviewing the background surveys that Standard & Poor's prepares on the more important industries. Perusal of trade publications and the statistical information available from trade associations should also prove useful.

After the company and industry data have been gathered and digested, the professional security analyst seeks to fill in the missing information gaps. Several key areas are normally discussed in any interview with corporate management (see some typical questions at the end of this section). It should be realized that the economic, government and industry winds blowing on a corporation often change direction swiftly. Companies are subject to such external developments as acts of God, release of government studies indicating that the materials used in the manufacture of its products are hazardous to health, and technological breakthroughs by competitors.

These fate factors are usually not subject to analysis. Therefore, we emphasize that the job of the analyst does not stop when the basic evaluation is made and that the subsequent follow-up work is of equal, and probably greater, importance.

Sales Trends

How much of the percentage increase in sales for the past year (past five years) was a function of unit growth and of price increases?

How much of that growth is attributable to new products?

What are the near, intermediate and long-term demand dynamics for your company's products?

Can you measure if the inventory level of the company's products has been building up at its distributors or at its ultimate users? If so, has it?

Are international sales important? If not, why not? If so, what geographic regions are the sales derived from?

What are the company's plans to boost the sales of a declining or problem product?

How is the advertising budget determined?

Are there any particularly important customers? How dependent is the company on any one (five, ten) customers?

Competition

Who are your most important competitors?

Is competition usually based on price, quality or service?

How are the company's products differentiated from those of the competition?

What are the barriers to entry into your industry?

Is there a lot of capacity coming on stream in your industry?

Is the company gaining or losing market share? If gaining, why? If losing, what is being done to reverse the situation?

Will the competitive environment permit an increase in prices?

Do you have any important patents that are due to expire soon? If so, what is the likely impact of this development?

Costs

Is the company categorized as a high-cost or low-cost producer?

What steps are being taken to increase efficiency and lower manufacturing costs?

What is the mix between raw material, labor and overhead costs?

What are the more important raw materials used? Does the company do any hedging to protect itself against dramatic short-term price swings? Is the company dependent on one or a few suppliers? How much are labor costs projected to rise?

Are any major new additions to capacity due to come on stream? Does the company anticipate experiencing any excessive start-up costs?

Labor

Are any labor contracts expiring this year?

What is the relationship between the union and the company?

Have there been many strikes in the past of long duration?

How are employees motivated?

Is employee turnover high? If so, why?

Finances

What are the company's projections for capital expenditures for this year and next?

Does the company need external financing? If so, how much?

Is the rate of return on investment increasing or decreasing? Why?

Is there a cash dividend payout objective?

What is the policy for stock dividends and/or splits?

Miscellaneous

Who follows the company in the investment community?

What can go wrong?

How much of the stock does management own?

PART TWO

ADVICE FROM THE PROS

Nine Lively Hints for Stock Market Success

ANN C. BROWN
*Chief Executive Officer,
A.C. Brown & Associates*

1. Be well informed. Ignorance definitely is not bliss when it comes to making and preserving money. Learn as much as you can about the companies you are invested in or thinking of investing in. Read and listen extensively to what is going on in the stock market, the economy, the country, and the world. If you haven't the time or the interest to keep abreast of the latest developments, follow the advice of someone who does.

2. Be flexible. Don't be afraid to admit you were wrong. If you sold a stock and new information makes it look attractive, buy the stock back, even if you have to pay a higher price. Similarly, if you didn't sell when you might have and things are looking dim for the stock, sell before it goes lower. We all make timing mistakes. Just don't compound them by failing to correct original errors promptly.

3. Keep emotion out of your stock decision-making process. Love your spouse, your children, but don't love your stocks. Just because they have been good to you in the past is no guarantee they will be good to you in the future. Similarly, don't dislike a certain stock or industry just because you once got burned. Today it may be the best buy around.

4. Don't outsmart yourself. By playing with eighth and quarter limits or stop-loss orders too close to the market, you can lose money. Also, beware of heavy margin positions and use options and short-selling only if you fully understand the risks you are taking.

5. Listen to takeover and merger rumors but consider the source. Only a handful of the hundreds of rumors you may hear become legitimate offers and fewer than that are actually completed. Buy each stock on its own merits. If someone later decides to buy the company, consider it an unexpected bonus.

6. Keep good records. Be careful not to let a short-term loss become a long-term loss unless you have a *very* good reason for doing so or you will lose a valuable tax advantage (consult your accountant). On the other hand, try to turn a short-term gain into a long-term gain wherever possible. Six months and a day seems like eternity in this short-term world, but hang in there the closer you get to long term. Even if the stock drops a bit, you could be ahead taxwise, by waiting.

7. Own only as many stocks as you can recite from memory. With most people, this is somewhere between eight and fifteen. Review your portfolio position once a week, if not daily. After ignorance, inattention is the second most deadly sin. Stocks are not a hobby like stamp collecting, which can be put away for a rainy Sunday. Unless you continually exercise your investment judgment, your portfolio can get out of shape very quickly.

8. Some miscellaneous observations: Look to buy what others are not buying. Use caution when buying stocks with big labor problems and big capital problems and stocks that are heavily regulated by the government. Be careful of inside information—an employee is not always the best judge of his own company's stock. Watch out for hot new "concept" stocks, which are here today and goners tomorrow. Be aware of stocks with an excessive amount of foreign earnings during these times when coups, nationalization, and expropriation are all too commonplace. Try to buy stocks that sell in double digits. Don't overconcentrate on any one stock—technological innovations, plant accidents, increased competition, raw material shortages, strikes, and so on can drop the price of a stock in a hurry.

9. Be lucky. There is no substitute for being in the right place at the right time or for doing the right thing for the wrong reason.

Get in Early and Have Patience

LOUIS EHRENKRANTZ

*Director,
Ehrenkrantz & King*

There are no "secrets" of investing that anyone can pass along (or choose to retain, for that matter) simply because there is no more public endeavor than the stock market. Every transaction is recorded for posterity, every industry is analyzed in depth, and every investment approach has its proponent. Yet, stock market mythology holds that there are those gurus who possess a system—a magic touch that ensures success.

My twenty-one years of experience have taught me otherwise: Some approaches work under certain circumstances but are ill-suited to others; no one approach works all the time. (If anything always worked, the market would soon correct itself to accommodate all those people who would invariably flock to partake of the "horn of plenty," and the effectiveness of the system would disappear.)

I think that the first thing any good money manager should do is set the limits and define the boundaries. I choose to be a long-term player, because that is the one aspect of investing that is bound by logical considerations. Long-term investing represents the most rational of universes, and is capable of being mastered. Short-term trading, on the other hand, is prone to too many irrational waves of emotion. All the activities connected with short-term investing (stop-loss orders, charting, etc.) stress following the lead of the market, rather than acting *in spite of* market behavior. The overriding factor in long-term investing is value, and value is determined away from the clamor of the market, "far from the madding crowd."

The ultimate value of a stock is determined by its earnings. Stripped of all rhetoric, that is what investing is all about. The short-term trader may try to capitalize on the rumor of a technological breakthrough, but the value-oriented investor tries to ascertain the following: Is the rumor true?, Will this breakthrough add to earnings progress?

I am one of those money managers stressing long-term growth who wants to be "the first kid on the block to own a toy," that is, I want to be early. I do not want to wait until a concept becomes popular before I buy. I am reminded of the axiom that one doesn't make money in crowds.

Being ahead of the crowd may reduce price risk, but it also means exercising more patience. If I am convinced that the crowd will follow, I'll stubbornly maintain an investment position until the other kids on the block find my toy so attractive that they'll want to own it. The short-term movement in any given stock may be irrational, but the ultimate price of a stock is governed by earnings progress.

Of course, if this kind of fundamental approach is to be effectively employed, one had better have good information and obtain it early. There are many ways to be well-informed, but I employ an approach reflecting my belief that even in our post-industrial society, contrary to expectations, it is technological innovation that sets one company above the other. Through a network of contacts in key academic areas, I keep abreast of changes in the basic areas of physics (laser technology), biology (genetic engineering and health care), and computer science. It is not generally appreciated how much the university has become the center of technological *change* as well as research: Silicon Valley owes its existence to the relationship between Frederick Terman, a Stanford professor, and his students: It was Terman who convinced his students, most notable among them William Hewlett and David Packard, to settle in the area and start their companies there. Genentech, leader in the genetic engineering industry, is located in San Francisco because of inventions developed at the local branch of the University of California. Similarly, the microprocessor industry owes much to the research conducted at M.I.T. In the post-industrial world, one had better monitor the academic world if one wants to be aware of fundamental changes that affect business decisions.

How to be early? Anticipatory research is best conducted in hidden corners—those out-of-the-way places where original contributions to technology are first discussed and where their commercial feasibility is examined. Scientific journals, trade magazines and journals of medicine are excellent sources of early information. Conversely, the worst places for anticipatory information-gathering are the daily newspapers and popular investment periodicals.

Indeed, it is easy to document that the financial pages are the most accurate barometer of investment peaks: By the time the major newspapers were heralding the "brave new world" that was to be ushered in by the proliferation of home computers, the shakeout had already begun. The shrillest point at which the dire predictions concerning the supposedly never-ending rise in the price of oil came just prior to the demise of the high-flying oil stocks in 1982. Shortly before the phenomenal bull market started in August 1982, America's most popular business magazine ran the presumptuous headline, "The Death of the Equities." Naturally, a portfolio of even not-so-carefully-chosen equities would have done quite well if bought in June 1982, all of which goes to prove that it is never as bad as the bears fear nor as good as the bulls proclaim.

I use a rather arcane method of monitoring the popular press. Since I think it is evident that the newspapers and magazines merely reflect conventional wisdom, reporting the consensus, I view a predominance of articles reflecting a given concern or attitude as a signal to act in a contrary manner. It is not merely that the majority is always wrong as much as it is that the reflection of a majority opinion offers no chance to anticipate a trend, which is the key to intelligent investing.

This intense monitoring of information likely to affect investment decisions is hardly a formal system, demanding as this discipline may be. It is merely a reflection of the belief—hardly original with me—that earnings determine stock prices, and it is best to anticipate earnings early on. I find the best way to be early is to ferret out the avant-garde in technological change.

Fear and Greed Rule the Market

WILLIAM M. LEFEVRE

*Vice President and Investment Strategiest,
Purcell, Graham & Co., Inc.*

There are only two emotions in Wall Street: fear and greed. Therein lies the basis for the psychology of the stock market. The market, far from stable, is in constant motion. It needs a force, and that force is buying and selling. "Buying sends them up, but selling knocks them down" is an old adage from the floor of the New York Stock Exchange. It is a demand-supply relationship. The supply of stocks is relatively fixed. Demand is the variable. Demand varies with the investor's sentiment, his feelings and emotions. He is sometimes hopeful or more. He is sometimes worrisome or worse.

The stock market has a life of its own. It leads a vicarious and reflective existance. It mirrors the feelings of the mass of investors and reacts to their stimuli. Because the market is largely based on credit, it tends to rise and fall on the availability or scarceness of funds. Thus, the stock market inhales money and exhales stocks.

It is a very emotional creature. Two people can conduct a rational discussion, but when three or more try the same thing, the discussion often becomes an emotional shouting match. The market behaves similarly: Mass psychology prevails; there is no gray, only black or white. That's why the only two emotions consistently exhibited in the stock market are fear and greed.

Greed demonstrates itself most clearly when the averages are making new highs. Otherwise intelligent investors know that they are about to pay too high a price for a stock, but they're afraid they'll miss out and can't bear to think of someone else making all that money. They are not unlike compulsive gamblers.

Fear, on the other hand, is most evident as the market falls toward newer new lows. The lower the market goes, the more bearish investors become. At these times, the public practically gives stocks away.

Real money is made by selling near the top and buying near the bottom. When everybody wants to sell a stock that has had a tremendous decline in price, that often is the time that some of the most profitable transactions can be initiated—by buying the stock nobody else wants, because the selling has probably been overdone, assuming there are some fundamentally sound reasons for the company to continue in business.

Conversely, when everybody wants to buy a stock, so much so that there doesn't seem to be a top in its price, that probably is the time to sell it. And, for the more venturesome, if you don't have any to sell, you can sell it short. Just as trees don't grow to the sky, stocks don't go up in price forever. There's always the Bigger Fool theory (I may be a fool to pay this high a price, but there's a bigger fool who'll pay me an even higher price tomorrow!). But those who play that game can wind up being the biggest fool—the buyer who paid the top eighth and then saw nothing but downticks—with no more foolish buyers left to take them out of the stock.

Much of the investing public, in this fear-and-greed syndrome, buys at the top, because their greed tells them the stock is going even higher, and they sell at the bottom, because their fear tells them there is no bottom. This is why the general public consistently loses in the market. This is also why large retail brokerage firms are constantly training new salesmen. Each market cycle cleans out another bunch of customers, and usually takes the customers' men with them.

Wall Street Syndromes: The Triumph of the Emotional over the Rational

ROBERT H. STOVALL

*Senior Vice President and Director of Portfolio Strategy,
Dean Witter Reynolds, Inc.*

Investing gives participants a mirror for their emotions: greed, doubt, avarice, altruism, hope, fear, and of course, pessimism. There is always a good living to be made by espousing pessimism. Just count the number of advertisements in next week's *Barron's* for market advices, index futures strategies, and precious metal/gem buying opportunities. Vendors with recent patches on their pants can consistently make a living of sorts telling other people how to get rich for a small fee. Just another sign that what dominates investors' action can frequently be the emotional rather than the rational.

I have spent much time over the last quarter-century lecturing around the world, pleading with investors to be, among other things, more rational and less emotional. To date, no noticeable success has been made. But I have picked up a number of syndromes that should not go unrecorded.

Take the Look East Young Man Syndrome. This is but a geographic extension of the belief that the fellow from the next town (or the last man off the airplane) is always more intelligent than you are. Wall Streeters, for example, have long admired the Scottish trust managers as being the canniest. Yet those money managers who ring Charlotte Square in Edinburgh are in awe of the Zurich gnomes, who in turn cannot restrain their admiration for the indestructible traders of The Levant, who are likewise building a grudging respect for the young bankers in Kuwait, who themselves have nothing but respect for the people in Hong Kong. As is well known, Hong Kong is a fast-growing center for commercial and investment banking. Yet those in Hong Kong by nature look East again to Honolulu, linked as it is by wire first with San Francisco and then Chicago and thus to New York for their particular requirements in the realm of financial acumen.

The complementary irrationality exists in the Look West Young Man Syndrome. In this reverse geographical search for the rationally irrational, we see recalled the American Dream. West is the place where the optimism is. It is not by accident that Continental and Scottish trusts wanted to invest in California in the years immediately following World War II. Because of the name, foreign investors even bought shares of California Packing (an earlier name for Del Monte, which has since been acquired by R.J. Reynolds), although much of the company's produce was grown in New Jersey.

There is also the Gravity Syndrome, which assumes that every stock that goes up must come down. Its mirror image is the Lighter Than Air Syndrome—what goes down must come up again. Or, what goes around, comes around. The Wild Blue Yonder Syndrome instructs investors that some stocks that rise have no limit to their ascent. This phenomenon rotates stock by stock and group by group.

Coloring one's judgment this way should not be confused with the Blue-Chip Syndrome, which is not geographic at all, and which persuades the afflicted that blue chips are the stuff of wisdom, forbearance, morality, and above all, good breeding. Those with Calvinist leanings are most often thus afflicted, believing that gains made from speculation must be ill-gotten, while profits from judicious, patient investment in blue chips are a just reward. Liberals believe inherited money is socially more acceptable than money earned by diligence and hard work. When wrong with market timing via a blue-chip portfolio, the investor goes "over the brink" first class, so to speak.

Perceptive observers of the market scene have noticed additional examples of decayed reasoning. Frequently isolated is the They Syndrome, which seeks a scapegoat in the collective personality. There is thus a "they" who makes the market go down: it is "they" who does the selling or produces the giant bid just after the individual has liquidated his position. At least one observer has made a career of blaming the NYSE specialists for most of what's wrong with the market—an all-encompassing "They." Then there is the practitioner of the Tag-Along Syndrome, who moves only when his friends do. This speculator feels better in company and is therefore the last in and the last out. This habit can prove expensive.

Widely held is the It's Not a Loss Until I Take It Syndrome. Investors who cannot accept a loss and won't liquidate for less than the purchase price let their losses run. Accepted wisdom is to let one's profits run and cut one's losses short. Practicing the reverse of this is tantamount to genocide for capital. Yet its practitioners would fill the Rose Bowl. Other millions suffer from the Lethargy Syndrome, whose followers believe that it may be wisest to leave poor enough alone—since things may get better if you do nothing.

Different legions are convinced of the Personality Syndrome, believing that stocks are people and have character and personality ("IBM has been good to me") and demand a personal loyalty. Another way of attaching personality to investments is to identify the good performers as being ideas of the investor (*my* winner), while the poor performers belong exclusively to the investment counselor or broker (*your* loser).

Many people take a position in an investment on the basis of a story they heard, which seemed to them rational when they heard it. Yet it might be even more rational to check out the story. Invest before you investigate is an all-too-frequent sequence of investment decision making and consequent money flows.

A personal test of your own rational irrationality can be found in the manner in which you appraise annual reports. Unemotional annual report dissectors read them as they would a Chinese newspaper, from the back forward. They digest and try to understand the footnotes to the financial statements before moving through the descriptions, financial summaries, and graphs. They save the photographs and the ebullience of the chairman's letter for last. Yet many investors make serious decisions on just the opposite basis. So many are motivated by the photos of management (e.g., the president is too old...he's too young...never invest in a company run by fat people...no women on the board) that such portraits are being omitted from an increasing number of reports. And how do you react when a company changes its name from a seasoned but no longer descriptive one to a cryptic string of letters, an acronym or a mnemonic? Most likely the earliest reaction is emotional. Let's hope it's not irrational.

How to Find Profits in Junior Growth Stocks

JOHN WESTERGAARD
President, Equity Research Associates, Inc.

There are two elements to investing in small growth companies. The first is to consider the basic reason why small growth companies have generally done well in recent years and the second is to formulate a strategy for successfully participating in the junior sector of the market.

There are ten basic, underlying reasons why small corporations have become increasingly "beautiful" in contrast to the corporate behemoths that constitute much of the U.S. economy:

1. Management. A highly educated managerial class with strong entrepreneurial instincts has emerged from the professional schools and certain key corporations over the past twenty years. These people often are more able than their counterparts in large corporations and are more willing to take risks.

2. Return on equity. Small corporations are generally able to realize higher returns on their shareholders' investment, which permits them to generate capital internally at a rapid rate. The average corporation in a portfolio of small growth stocks might generate 20–25 percent net after taxes on shareholders' equity, compared with 15 percent for the average U.S. corporation.

3. Flexibility. Small corporations have greater flexibility to move with changing times and economic circumstances.

4. Diversity. As the U.S. and world economy becomes increasingly pluralistic, the opportunities for small companies to establish positions in emerging "niche industries" increases. Big companies often don't see these market opportunities until they are well on their way to development.

5. Human scale. Small companies, by definition, function on a scale that is more personalized than large corporations. They are often able to attract better employees for this reason.

6. Social trends. Evolving social patterns in the 1960s and 1970s favored smallness over bigness, and these trends are likely to continue through the 1980s. Shifting public attitudes favoring the theme "small is beautiful" have affected (a) how investors view small companies, (b) where better-educated, more venturesome young people might choose to seek employment, and (c) how capital is allocated within the private sector and between the private and public sectors.

7. Government. Attempts by the government to exert price controls over the corporate sector have employed the "trickle down" theory, whereby regulations are imposed upon the 1000 largest corporations, leaving smaller companies with freer hands.

8. Mobility. Small companies normally have greater ability to move operations in order to take advantage of better labor pools, better tax jurisdictions, the myriad of incentives offered by various communities to attract capital investment, and so forth.

9. Capital. Contrary to conventional wisdom, in recent years smaller companies have had an easier time raising capital on attractive terms than have large corporations. Equity markets have been receptive to new issues of small growth companies.

10. International. As small companies reach the $30–$50 million level, they typically enter foreign markets and often experience accelerating growth at a time when one might normally expect growth to slow down. The typical U.S. technology company does 40 percent more of its business overseas.

So much for the fundamental reasons why small companies are outperforming big ones. Equally important is the question of strategy. How should one approach investing in these kinds of companies?

First, one should focus on the kinds of companies with which one is comfortable. If one does not feel at home with high-technology stocks, usually associated with high market volatility, then skip them. There are many opportunities in what we like to refer to as "Swamp Yankee Middle America Appleknocker" stocks, namely Middle America-type companies that may not be superglamorous but that have a secure niche in a basic business.

Second, in buying small growth stocks, timing is of key importance. To be successful over the longer term requires being something of a contrarian and exercising patience. One must be prepared to buy smaller company stocks when they are out of favor or before they are discovered. Once they become market favorites, it usually pays to step aside. Almost inevitably, fast-growing, smaller companies will run into a "blip" at some point in the course of their operations, and the patient investor will have a second chance to step in and buy the stock cheaply.

Be careful of fads and be careful of companies that are heavily pushed by many brokers and where there are large institutional holdings. One should buy before the institutions get in, and that is surprisingly easy to do. Very few institutions will buy stock in companies with less than $20 million in market value, and many companies selling for less than that in aggregate value can be found if one looks hard enough. Eventually, if they grow, these institutions will discover them. Then it is important to exercise patience a second time—don't be too quick to sell. If the selection process was well applied to begin with, it usually pays to stick with the winners.

Seven Golden Rules on How to Beat the Market —Again and Again and Again

YALE HIRSCH

Editor, Stock Trader's Almanac

1. Contrary opinion. This is Number One of all stock market disciplines. If you've got contrarian instincts, we can almost guarantee investment success. While Norman Vincent Peale made a fortune from *The Power of Positive Thinking,* if you want to make it in the market, learn the Power of Contrary Thinking. When everything is dark, bleak, and impossible, it usually is time to buy stock.

2. Market timing. If you've got a good sense of market timing and can handle short-term overbought/oversold indicators or timing cycles, telephone switching between a money market fund and a maximum-performance mutual fund can be your best bet. It saves time by eliminating the need to select individual stocks. Or you can work with a select group of stocks you are familiar with, by switching from long to short positions back and forth several times a year.

3. Hedging. This is the best way to beat the market with virtually no risk at all by simultaneously buying and selling two different securities whose values are linked, in order to take advantage of any price discrepancies. Another name for it is *arbitrage*. Buying convertible bonds that are selling at a discount while shorting the underlying stock is one form of hedging.

4. Insider transactions. These provide the most academically proven, successful stock-selection systems on record. Even well-known "random walkers" will acknowledge that this is one way to beat the market. There are, besides the SEC, a number of services that provide the raw data. Others select companies to buy or sell, using certain parameters.

5. New issues. They have been described as the closest thing to a sure thing Wall Street has to offer by those who follow them. When the market is hot or even lukewarm, most solid new issues immediately go to a premium, especially high-technology companies. Certain underwriters have sensational batting averages. The difficulty, of course, is getting your broker to give you an allocation of the most promising new issues. And the danger is that when a new-issue boom develops, many stocks of little or no value are put out along with the worthwhile ones.

6. Technical analysis. This can be a very handy aid when it comes to stock selection. Though academicians claim that charts do not work, I don't agree. When someone tells me about a chart, I can see a mountain of information by glancing at its chart. Robert Levy of Computer Directions in Silver Spring, Maryland, sums it up succinctly: "Charts not only tell what WAS, they tell what IS. And a trend from WAS to IS (projected linearly into the WILL BE) contains better percentages than clumsy guessing."

7. Risk arbitrage. This provides the greatest rewards the stock market has to offer, as far as I know. It usually involves taking a position on whether an announced merger will or will not take place. Annual appreciation of over 100 percent is not uncommon. To be successful, however, one must know a lot about the securities industry and federal and state laws and be willing to work long hours at it.

A Not-so-Random Walk to Stock Market Profits

EUGENE D. BRODY

*Senior Vice President
and Director of Option Management,
Oppenheimer Capital Corp.*

In a classic article on Ted Williams many years ago in *Sports Illustrated*, the great Red Sox slugger said the record he was most proud of was "most bases on balls." The surprised interviewer queried Williams on why this was so. Williams replied that it proved that he had the patience and discipline to wait for the pitch he wanted before he swung.

Stock market investors would do well to practice a similar patience and discipline. Assuming that the objective of stock ownership is profit and not excitement, then investors should learn to wait for the market's "fat pitch" in order to hit home runs. These fat pitches occur infrequently, but they are identifiable. They last for several months and generally fly in the face of all the investment advice being offered at the time. Buying stocks at these times might seem foolhardy if one's buying decision was based on the media's recap of the problems of the day. Pay no heed. It is time to swing.

How can we identify these golden opportunities? First, let us use hindsight. In each decade, there appear to be a small number of periods that were the obvious times to purchase stocks. A casual perusal of a stock market chart will clearly show that in the post-war period, the time to be buying stocks was mid-1947, mid-1949, late-1957, mid-1962, late-1966, mid-1970, late-1974, early-1978, and mid-1982.

Having identified the opportune periods, we must find some common denominator that they all share and that does not include any other periods. There is just such a common denominator. It is the year-to-year rate of change of the S&P 500. Every one of these periods could be identified at the time when this indicator crossed over the −10 percent mark. That moment in time did not pinpoint the absolute bottom, but marked the beginning of what always turned out to be near enough to the bottom to be considered an area of opportunity. The six months following the crossing has always included the absolute bottom.

An intelligent stock buying program would be to spread purchases out (through dollar averaging) over the ensuing six months. The greatest percentage gains on these purchases seem to occur within two years of the purchase (see Figure 1). In some cases, stocks continued to advance for a longer period but the gains after two years were never as great as the period up to two years.

As to which stocks to buy, the average investor would probably do best buying a package of mutual funds. My own preference would be two or three growth stock funds with assets of under $150 billion. They will be almost sure to participate, are not unwieldly for the managers and have the greatest chance to attract new investors as the market rises, which is a positive performance factor.

What has been outlined here is not a magic formula for money making. It is a discipline designed to increase the odds in the investor's favor by showing him how to wait for and recognize the fat pitch. Most professionals do not beat the market averages and most stock market investors do not even earn fair returns. The basic reason for this is that they do not buy low and sell high. They buy high and expect to sell higher to the greater fool. Then they find out they are the fool.

FIGURE 1
The S&P 500 Annual Rate of Change

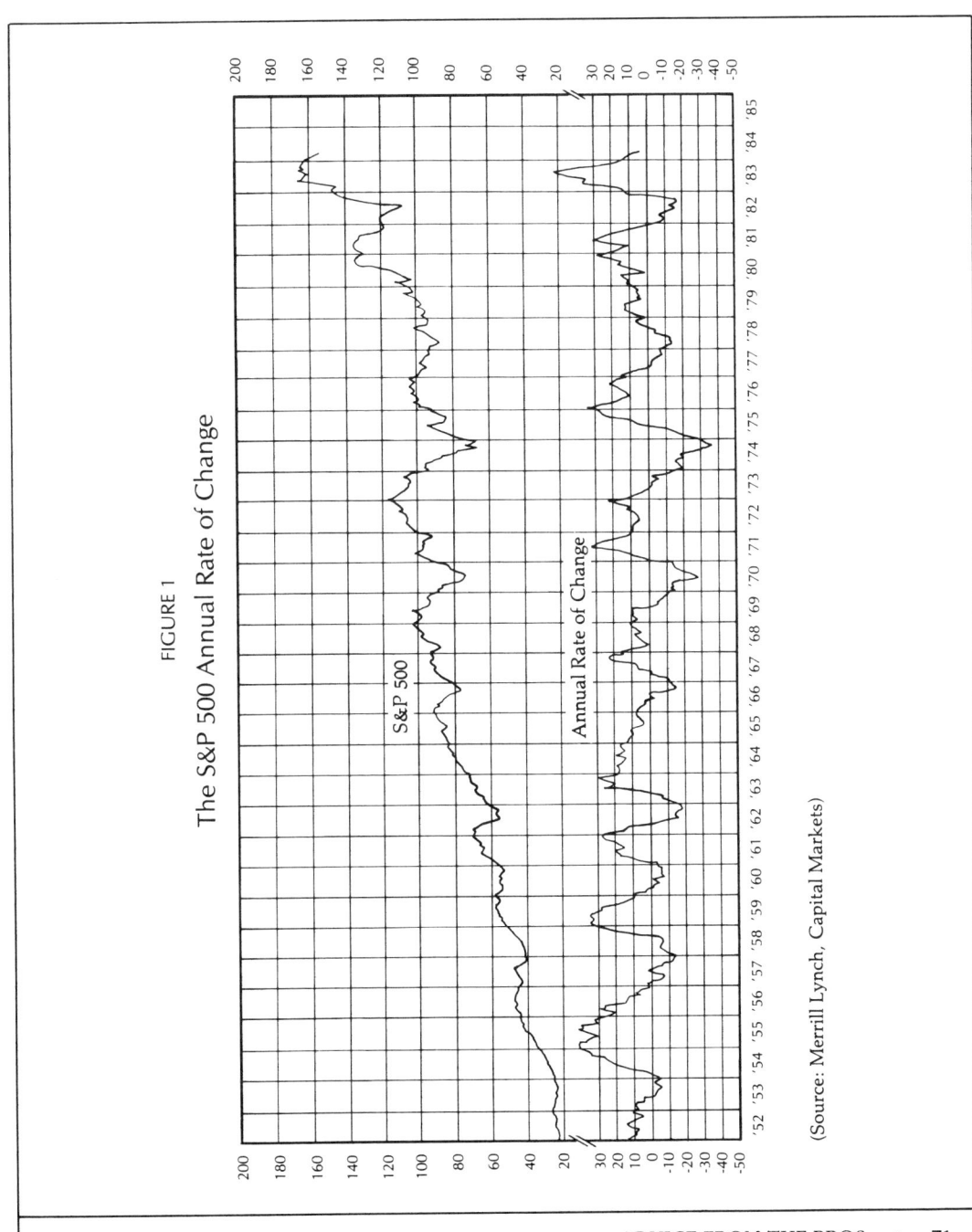

(Source: Merrill Lynch, Capital Markets)

Invest With Your Head —Not With the Herd

JAMES BALOG

*Senior Executive Vice President,
Drexel Burnham Lambert Inc.*

Everybody knows, or should know, that the market is ruled by greed and fear. The volatility of the market over the years has proved that point, and recent times have put a sharp point on that observation. One thing I have learned about fear and greed is that fear is *temporary* while greed is *permanent.* It has always amazed me that investors can be burned in a given situation, but their memories are so short that they come back to it again and again. It is not that there's a new crop of investors that take the second and third swing. It's the same people who do it over and over again. This behavior leads me to the conclusion that the persistence of greed determines it.

The explanation for the persistence of greed and the temporary nature of fear can perhaps be found in the psychology of mass behavior. Related to that is the role of cool, calculating, fundamental securities analysts. One would expect that analysts making astute reviews of the financial statements, calling on the companies, understanding industries and technologies, and utilizing sophisticated computer technologies would be immune to mass psychology. But over and over again, I've seen earnings estimates being increased by analysts as stock prices rise. Conversely, earnings estimates are cut as the stock price falls. Typically, the earnings estimates on Wall Street are at their peak just before the crash of a company's fortunes, in the near term at least.

In trying to figure out why this happens, I've concluded that it probably relates to the fact that analysts are both too close to the companies and too highly specialized by industry. In short, they tend to get caught up in the same euphoria that afflicts company managements—especially in the high-tech, high-growth industries.

Putting together the fear, the greed, and the earnings estimate behavior of the fundamental analyst, leads to the one great wisdom that I have learned. *Be a contrarian.* It's very easy to get caught up in the euphoria of a rising stock and very difficult to go against the grain.

And yet, there are times when simple arithmetic can give obvious clues to the contrarian. For example, there were times when some of the high-tech companies were growing at such a rapid rate that they were discounting earnings ten years or more into the future. And yet, if they grew at that rate for ten years, their total revenues would be greater than the nation's total gross national product, or close to it. Clearly, there was something unreal about the expectations. These are the times when the contrarian has to make his move.

There have been some very interesting studies showing the investment results from selling the ten stocks with the highest price/earnings multiples in the Dow Jones Industrial Average and buying the ten lowest P/E stocks on a consistent schedule. Doing that consistently and mindlessly quarter after quarter, generates better performance than searching the list on some esoteric grounds.

In short, the stocks that are selling at high multiples have high expectations and have nowhere to go but down, while the stocks "nobody loves" will again be loved. Sometimes, one will miss the rest of a move upward. But I have found that it's better to wait around until the industry or stock has its inevitable correction, watch how the management handles adversity, and then catch it on the next wave. This is particularly true of very unseasoned companies. It is when a company falls upon hard times that one can distinguish between fallen angels that will reward your faith and the Streetwalkers that won't. Succinctly put, invest with your head and not with the herd.

Financial Deregulation and Its Impact on Deflationary Economic Growth and Profits in the Stock and Bond Markets

ARNOLD X. MOSKOWITZ

Senior Vice President and Economist,
Dean Witter Reynolds, Inc.

The economy has entered an environment never seen before by investors —a disinflationary cycle that is largely the result of financial deregulation. This new cycle, which could see the base rate of inflation, as measured by wage rates, declining to 2 percent by the end of the decade, is an important consequence of the financial deregulation that began in the late 1970s and culminated in the Monetary Control Act of 1980. It already has had a significant impact on economic activity, and it is forcing a major structural change in the financial markets. Its implications are as far-reaching as the OPEC oil shocks of the mid-1970s.

Few observers have understood all the ramifications of financial deregulation as it has unfolded, but a number of salient conclusions are now clear:

- The phenomenon of high real interest rates (meaning after inflation is factored out) is the result of monetary decontrol. Real interest rates on bonds will permanently range in the 6–8 percent zone for the next several years, while bond rates will decline irregularly.

- Real asset prices, such as those for oil, gold, and real estate, will stagnate or decline.

- The returns on financial assets will significantly outpace inflation.

- Additions of new long-term debt leverage will be a major burden on the companies and individuals that incur them.

- Moderate unit volume growth will force new product development if companies are to prosper.

- Market share battles will intensify and more industry concentration will result in some big winners.

- Variable cost control and lower break-even points will be an essential strategy for companies in mature industries.

- International competition will rise, especially in the United States, as a strong dollar allows greater levels of cheap imports, with the likely result being more protectionist legislation.

The Start of a New Era

Monetary deregulation began rather innocuously in 1978, when the government allowed money market mutual funds to be sold to small investors and also permitted the thrifts and savings banks to issue six-month money market certificates in $10,000 denominations. The reason for this latter development was to enable the thrift industry to attract additional funds for the housing industry during times of high interest rates.

In 1981, a scheduled phase-out of the regulated interest rate ceilings on most certificates of deposit began. Furthermore, thrifts were allowed to pay interest on checking account balances (NOW accounts). Presently, there are SuperNOW and money market deposit accounts—and more deregulation is yet to come for business checking accounts. Therefore, for the first time since the 1940s, savers were given an opportunity to obtain high yields on their savings comparable to those returns available to large institutions.

The major disadvantage of deregulation, however, is that it dramatically raised the banking industry's cost of obtaining funds. In the old days of financial regulation, the banks' cost of deposits for checking account balances was zero, and savings accounts paid 5¼ percent on passbooks. In the deregulated environment, NOW accounts (used for checking) cost the banks about 5 percent in interest paid, and six-month certificates, which are equivalent to money market rates, range about 4–5 percentage points above the base rate of inflation. This means that with a 5 percent inflation rate, six-month certificates yield 9–10 percent, which is 4–5 percentage points above the old 5¼ passbook rate. Therefore, the cost of acquiring funds for banks has risen 4–5 percentage points above the costs before deregulation.

As a consequence, the banks pass the higher cost of obtaining short-term funds on to the users of debt through higher bank loan rates. For example, consumer installment loan rates, which were 11 percent in the early 1970s, rose to 15–16 percent in the deregulated environment of the early 1980s. Furthermore, this rise in costs was also translated into higher longer-term mortgage loan costs.

While the phenomenon of rising costs is clear for the banking industry, much the same upward cost shift has affected the capital markets. The credit market has maturities stretching from three months to 30 years. (The yield curve in normal times sets returns based upon the short-term rates. Bond rates usually yield 2–3 percentage points more (given present yield levels) as the necessary premium to induce lenders to hold long-term obligations).

In the inflationary period of the 1970s, investors received a negative return on their bond investments, but in the present deregulated environment they require positive returns. In terms of estimating the premium between short- and long-term rates, this can be analyzed using a real after-tax return: If the individual investor has to be bribed to save more, he needs high returns in order to forego spending and to save instead. Moreover, while it is reasonable to expect a zero return on cash equivalent assets, the case for the bondholder requires at least 1 percent real after-tax returns, since historical studies have shown that real pre-tax returns have been 2-3 percent. In the case of the bondholder, if we start with an 8 percent inflation rate assumption, 12 percent for short-term rates, and now add 2 percent for the bond premium for the investor, we get a 14 percent yield. At 14 percent, the average investor with a marginal tax rate of 33 percent will get a 1.4 percent real after-tax return.

This calculation was arrived at in a straightforward manner—if the inflation rate is 8 percent, the spread above the inflation rate for short-term rates is 4 percent, and, if a 2 percent bond premium is added to short-term rates, we get the 14 percent corporate bond rate. If the tax rate is 33 percent, the individual pays 4.6 percent to the government for taxes and his after-tax return is 9.4 percent. If the effects of 8 percent inflation are subtracted, the individual is left with a real after-tax return of 1.4 percent. Therefore, as a rough rule of thumb, if an investor wanted to calculate the expected yields on high-grade corporate bonds (in order to get a 1.5 percent real after-tax return), he should double the expected inflation rate. For example, a 6 percent inflation rate should yield a 13 percent bond yield.

The Outlook for the Capital Markets

In this environment, the outlook for the credit markets is highly favorable to investors. In regard to interest rates, mid-1982 saw the cyclical peak in bond yields, with high-grade AA utility bonds yielding 16 percent (30-year Treasury bonds yielded 14.2 percent). These corporate bond rates should trend irregularly lower as the underlying rate of inflation declines from 8 percent to 4 percent by mid-1985. In the bond market, high real interest rates will remain the hallmark of this cycle. By 1988, with the inflation rates down to 3 percent, high-grade AA utility bonds should decline to 10 percent from the 1982 peaks.

In this high real interest disinflationary environment, there are some clear implications for corporate profitability in the years ahead. The factors we would use to sort out the successful companies from the others in the equity market fit into five categories:

1. Avoid companies that have a significant amount of short-term debt on their balance sheets, because the rollover of this debt into the long-term market will be very costly. Conversely, high internal profits and cash-flow generation will give companies greater flexibility to invest either for expansion internally or through acquisitions externally on favorable terms.

2. Avoid companies that achieved their profits growth in the past cycle through price increases. Clearly, in a disinflationary environment profits growth will come from volume increases rather than price boosts.

3. Therefore, look for strong unit-volume increases. However, the economy in general will show moderate growth (real gross national product gains of 3–4 percent) since important sectors will have sub-par growth —for example, capital spending, exports, state, and local spending, housing, and autos. As a result, growth stocks in both the consumer and technology areas that can leverage their earnings up, based upon their individual product cycles, will be favorably situated. They will be relatively immune to the economic cycle if they can avoid the use of debt to maintain growth, and companies that can innovate with new product development will succeed even more. Another way profits and unit volume growth can be achieved is through market share gains, which in some cases will occur at the expense of weak competitors. For example, in the deregulated industries of trucking and airlines, as well as a mature industry such as farm equipment, the dominant companies will remain.

4. Ability to control costs. For some mature industries like autos, substantial price increases are unlikely, and volume gains will be purely cyclical. However, these companies will have to control variable costs—labor and materials—to survive. This appears to be occurring now, and operating leverage will then work in their favor. Another industry that will need to control costs is banking. Here, the money center banks that operate soundly (and don't have significant foreign loans) and use spread banking and liability management, should do well. Well-run regional banks will dominate their weak competitors, and mergers or takeovers will be the rule for the strong ones as the effect of financial deregulation is felt. Likewise, weaker regional banks that have a significant proportion of their deposits in passbooks (which will rollover into six-month certificates) or those that have a significant amount of their revenues tied to fixed-rate assets (mortgages) will not have control of their costs and probably will not survive.

5. The international arena. In my view, high real interest rates are likely to keep the dollar relatively strong for several years. This implies that export industries will find a difficult environment in which to operate; multinational companies' profits will continue to be under pressure from negative currency translation effects; and import competition in the U.S. market will intensify, as cheaper-priced imports have a favorable currency advantage. As these problems surface, there is likely to be more trade restrictions to protect domestic industries, especially against countries whose home markets are not open to the full range of U.S. export products. Therefore, industries such as steel should benefit.

In conclusion, the range of opportunities in this new environment are plentiful. Investors and companies aware of the new financial landscape and prepared to face the onslaught of disinflation will succeed. Those companies that are set to fight the last war—inflation—will suffer the same fate as the Maginot Line builders; that is, they will be overrun by a new reality.

Ehrlich's Cardinal Rules of Investing

HAROLD B. EHRLICH

Chairman Emeritus, Bernstein-Macaulay, Inc.

1. *Don't ever lose a lot of money.* The simple arithmetic behind this proposition is that it takes a 50 percent gain to compensate for a 33 percent loss, and a 100 percent gain to compensate for a 50 percent loss.

2. *Stay with your style of investing.* This proposition is based upon the old adage of doing what you do best. Specifically, if you employ an investment approach with which you do not feel comfortable, you multiply the odds of making mistakes.

3. *No one class of assets is the best type of investment for all times.* For example, technology stocks were wonderful vehicles in the mid and late 1960s, as they were again during 1979 and 1980. However, there was a long dry spell in between, when funds might have been better employed elsewhere.

4. *Maintain your investment options and opportunities.* In other words, always be willing to survey the entire field of investments for new opportunities, and don't become emotionally "hung up" on any specific kind of investment.

5. *Make big bets and watch them carefully.* Excessive diversification

will not protect against major losses in the marketplace when the whole market is going down. Conversely, when the market is going up, an excessively diversified portfolio, by definition, is unlikely to outperform the market. The same concept holds for investing in any kind of asset. Research carefully, take concentrated positions, and re-examine those positions frequently.

The Federal Reserve Plays the Music—and All the Financial Markets Dance to Its Tune

DAVID M. JONES

*Senior Vice President and Economist,
Aubrey G. Lanston & Co., Inc.*

The Federal Reserve (the Fed) has become perhaps the single most dominant influence on the financial markets. This impact is particularly evident in the domestic stock and bond markets, but, remarkably, Fed actions currently reign supreme in the foreign exchange markets as well.

The Fed's influence on the domestic and foreign financial markets became most pronounced in the fateful period from October 1979 to October 1982. In that three-year period, the monetary authorities, in line with their anti-inflation objectives, sought to more effectively limit monetary growth, while, at the same time, tolerating unusually wide fluctuations in interest rates. Accordingly, this period saw the Federal funds rate (the rate on reserve balances traded among banks, usually overnight) fluctuate wildly from a low of 8.68 percent to a high of 20.06 percent. The funds rate is the most sensitive of any interest rates to Fed policy shifts and, as such, serves as the anchor for other key money market rates, such as the prime rate.

The acute responsiveness of the financial markets to Fed policy moves continued in 1983–1984. For example, it was the aggressive Fed easing of bank reserve pressures and the associated downward pressure on interest rates in the final months of 1982 that apparently provided the main thrust for the huge stock and bond market rallies of late 1982 early 1983. Over this same period, the Fed's easing moves contributed to a decline in the value of the U.S. dollar on the foreign exchange market as foreigners found the declining relative rates on U.S. investments less attractive.

The financial markets' sensitivity to Fed policy shifts was still more recently evident when the monetary officials—in pursuit of the economic objective of moderate growth with continued low inflation—moved, in May 1983, to moderately tighten bank reserve pressures. As a result, in the second half of 1983, there were related increases to about 9½ percent from 8½ percent in the Federal funds rate and to roughly 12 percent from 10½ percent in the longer-term Treasury bond rate. These Fed firming actions stopped the stock market rally in its tracks. This was because investors found rising interest rates on alternative investments increasingly attractive and because it was feared that rising rates would eventually depress economic growth and thus reduce profit prospects. At the same time, this Fed tightening move and related upward pressure on interest rates, pushed the value of the U.S. dollar to record highs in late 1983 as foreigners shifted funds into U.S. dollar investments carrying increasingly attractive rates, especially relative to rates on foreign investments.

Thus, as a general rule, it can be expected that when the Fed tightens bank reserve pressures and exerts upward pressure on U.S. interest rates both the stock and bond markets will weaken, while the foreign exchange value of the U.S. dollar will strengthen. Conversely when the monetary authorities move to ease bank reserve pressures and to exert downward pressure on interest rates, the stock and bond markets will rally, while, at the same time, the U.S. dollar will decline.

As a practical matter, investors should be on the lookout for the slightest signs that the Fed has decided—perhaps in response to excessive economic or monetary growth—to tighten bank reserve pressures. Such signs that the Fed has clamped down on the supply of bank reserves will usually first appear at the Fed discount window. A Fed decision to squeeze bank reserves might force banks, for example, to *increase* their borrowings at the discount window by $250–$500 million, averaged over a five-to-seven-week period. In this case, stock and bond market investors should beware. Conversely, if the Fed should move to ease pressures on bank reserves—perhaps in response to shortfalls in economic or monetary growth—there would likely be a like-sized *decline* in bank borrowings at the discount window. In that case, stock and bond market investors should take heart.

Finding Profits in Troubled Situations

MONTE J. GORDON
Vice President and Director of Research, Dreyfus Corporation

A collection of all the theories for investment success undoubtedly would run the alphabetical gamut from *A* to *Z*. I favor settling on the letter *T*, standing, as in the famous song from *The Music Man*, for *trouble*—or for *turnaround*, which is another side of the same coin.

When you invest in troubled or turnaround situations, what you really are doing is putting your judgment against that of the stock market. You are betting that the current state of market disfavor has resulted in a substantial undervaluation of the security in question. Sometimes, perfectly sound companies are simply being overlooked by the market. Advantageous purchases in those cases mean taking your position before the market corrects its error and the price of the stock rises to its appropriate level.

The troubled situation is different, since it may involve a company that has been generally well regarded in the past but has fallen on difficult times. Here the level of analysis required is somewhat higher because it calls for an evaluation of the trouble. The risk is that the investor's perception can be mistaken. If correct, however, the rewards often can be substantial. Indeed, the overall risk may be mitigated by the fact that the issue has declined significantly in price because of the trouble and can be bought at a low price historically.

Neither of these approaches, while sound in principle, is easy of execution when one is confronted with the reality of decision. They demand not only conviction of judgment, but patience to await recognition by the market of the values which you have perceived. And, once recognized, the situation will only advance as the knowledge spreads and comes to the attention of a widening group of investors. At that point, the last caveat —don't overstay your welcome. When your values have been reached by the market, curb your greed and don't yield to the siren song of still more. In short, don't hesitate to sell.

Cashing In on Unexpected Developments

MICHAEL J. JOHNSTON

President, Paine Webber Capital Markets Group, Inc.

People buy stocks to make money. In order to make money in a stock, one or more of several events should occur: Stock market levels generally rise; the industry sector of which the company is a part does surprisingly well; the individual company surprises investors with better-than-expected earnings, better-than-expected dividends, an unexpected new product or discovery, or some other unanticipated event that bodes well for the company, such as a change in taxation or regulation.

The words that recur throughout the events that make stocks rise are "surprisingly," "unexpected," "unanticipated." Except for a general rise in stock prices, investors must foresee the unexpected in order to make money.

The art of forecasting the unexpected is very difficult and complex, and generally must be based on the work of skilled professionals. Nevertheless, two simple rules can aid in better investing. One rule is to buy into accelerating earnings trends, such as +5 percent, +10 percent, +15 percent, on a quarterly earnings comparison basis or annual earnings basis. There is no certainty of a trend continuing, but comparisons such as this indicate something surprisingly good is occurring. And the stock market often lags in its full appreciation of these earnings.

The other simple rule is a willingness to think differently about an industry or company. If the media are reporting the problems of a company, and if one has reason to think the problems are at their worst, then future developments may begin to surprise investors in a favorable way. Obviously, the willingness to think differently must be based on informed judgment regarding future events. Some refer to this rule as a "contrary opinion," but the important element is that "opinion" must be reasoned. Simple "contrarians" can make painful mistakes.

Minimizing Downside Risk by Allocating the Asset Mix

MARTIN D. SASS

President, M.D. Sass Investors Services, Inc.

Investors should strive to achieve a consistent superior "real" rate of return within a pre-determined amount of risk, as opposed to seeking to "beat the market." In order to accomplish this objective, one should invest "defensively" by minimizing the downside volatility of investment portfolios. The sharp market declines of 1969–1970, 1973–1974, 1977, 1981, and early 1984 proved that superior investment performance resulted from preserving gains achieved during rising markets from erosion in declining markets. The arithmetic underlying the need for "defensive" investing is simple: If a portfolio loses 20 percent in one year, it must rise by 53 percent in the following year merely to keep pace in real terms with an 11 percent annual inflation rate over the two-year period.

Probably the single most important means of reducing downside volability is the active allocation of assets among equities, fixed-income securities, short-term cash equivalents, and other investments (e.g., real estate, oil and gas, options and financial futures). Although I believe that securities prices are in a long secular uptrend, I expect both the equity and fixed-income markets to be extremely volatile and fast-moving for the foreseeable future. This forecast is based on the likelihood of continued economic and political problems and uncertainties. Along with this expected continued market volatility, however, will be exceptional capital gains opportunities for the investor equipped to actively change the allocation of his investments among different types of investment and different sectors of the financial markets.

In addition to using traditional analytic methods and judgment, investors can employ computer-based techniques to assist in the various stages of the investment process: asset allocation, market-sector weighting, and specific security selection. The use of quantitative tools is proliferating; improved methods of forecasting investment risk and return are being developed by innovative investment professionals to provide a more systematic, reliable, and internally consistent methodology to the investment process. These computerized quantitative techniques, while useful tools, are of course not a substitute for the key to successful investing: sound investment judgment.

Every investment strategy should employ a "sell discipline." The biggest problem among investors is that they fail to utilize soundly conceived sell disciplines after buying a security. Before I buy a stock for any client of our investment-management firm, I establish a predetermined "review for sale price." My firm has historically sold the security about 80 percent of the time when it hits that target (the remaining 20 percent of the time we adjust the sale target due to a change in the outlook for the company or the market). The process is similar on the downside. If a stock's price drops 15 percent, we review the company's outlook, and the decision is made either to buy more or to sell the security.

The Topsy-Turvy World of Investing: Conservatism Versus Speculation

PIERRE A. RINFRET

President, Rinfret Associates, Inc.

What is conservative today? What is speculation? Times change, and so do definitions. "Conservative" investors today are in fact speculators, and the "speculators" are conservatives.

In the historical sense, the conservative investor was one who worked to conserve existing capital rather than create more capital. This was done largely by investing in long-term debt instruments that had excellent interest-payment coverage and a rather superb issuer balance sheet that assured (in theory) the ability to pay off or refinance the debt at maturity.

A trust officer, as defined by the courts over the years, was a person who bought the same securities other trust officers bought. The courts, time and time again, looked to the rule of the prudent investor, which said, in essence, that if all or mostly all trust officers are doing this, it must be prudent. The action of the population of trust officers was the thing.

Common stocks were riskier than bonds. For one thing, their price fluctuated a great deal. For another thing, they had no claim on earnings, while debt instruments did. Stocks are nonredeemable and depend for yield and price largely on the future course of earnings.

The speculator risked capital. The conservative investor did not risk capital or minimized the risks to that capital. The conservative investor *thought* he had guarded capital. He did it by:

1. Investing in long-term debt instruments with a known maturity, a relatively assured yield, and a relatively assured price in the open market.

2. Purchasing preferred stocks that had tax advantages, a high yield relative to common stocks but lower yield than debt instruments, and some modest possibilities of capital appreciation.

3. Investing in high-yield common stocks whose dividends were well covered by the "defensive" industries. Investments in alcohol and tobacco stocks were considered safe investments because their earnings did not go down in recessions (in fact, they frequently rose then).

4. Investing in industries that produced the essentials of life but that were neither "growth" nor cyclical" industries. These industries were not terribly vulnerable to business corrections, nor did their growth rate accelerate during business expansion.

This conservative policy began to fall apart in 1966. How conservative has conservative policy been since 1966?

In 1966 the prime rate was 6 percent. At this writing, it is under 11 percent, having been as high as 20½ percent in 1980. Long-term bonds have had material up-and-down cycles around a declining price trend. The investor who held long-term bonds in 1966 was faced with these alternatives in the subsequent years: (1) sell his bonds at a loss; (2) pray for an up cycle; (3) hold his bonds to maturity. By any standard, the long-term bondholder of 1966 has seen his capital wither away since then. Long-term bonds have been a total failure in the preservation of capital, particularly if we talk about the preservation of real capital.

In 1966 the Dow Jones Industrial Average topped 1000 very briefly. It hit 1051 in early 1973, and, in July 1984, after one of the biggest bull markets in history, it was 1086. Investments in the solid companies of the Dow (e.g., DuPont, Eastman Kodak, U.S. Steel, General Motors) have produced a dividend yield for the past fifteen years but virtually no capital gains (assuming that the ability to buy at the bottom and sell at the top has existed only in a mathematical model, because it doesn't exist much in fact).

What we hve today is a vast legacy of outmoded, outdated "conservative" policies in investment management that have been, in fact, unbelievably speculative. Why have these conservative policies been speculative? Because the so-called conservative policies have assumed that:

1. Interest rates would not rise over time.

2. Inflation would not accelerate and would, in fact, be beaten down.

3. The well-established giants would maintain their positions of preeminence, and domestic competition would not erode their market shares.

4. Foreign competition was and would be of little or no concern.

5. Peace and tranquility would prevail in the world.

6. And many other assumptions.

The so-called conservative investor assumed that all was for the best in the best of all possible worlds. He assumed that everything would work out fine. He assumed that the world would follow the old rules. He was and is a speculator. He bets on everything working out fine. He bets against the odds.

Today the so-called speculator pursues a different set of rules. He actually follows a conservative path:

1. He keeps his debt instruments invested short-term. He knows that monetary policy is volatile and the only way to protect capital is to keep it liquid, to refuse to commit it to the uncertainties of the market. He refuses to speculate on long-term trends and is clearly unwilling to bet on the longer-term future.

2. He purchases the common stocks of corporations whose earnings are growing about 25–35 percent per year on a per-share basis. He wants a real growth in earnings and counts on that real growth to return dividends to him.

3. He is willing to forego dividends today for growth tomorrow. He understands that profits reinvested in a company "assure" the future growth of the company and that dividend payments are an inefficient use of capital.

4. He avoids preferred securities because he makes pure plays.

The "speculator" has built into his policy some extremely conservative biases. He assumes that:

1. We live in a highly volatile, almost unpredictable world.

2. Cutting-edge technology is the wave of the present and the safety net of the future.

3. Monetary and fiscal policy are erratic.

4. There are no certainties or near-certainties, there are only odds.

We live in a topsy-turvy world. We need to re-examine the rules we follow. Changing times have passed by what used to be the traditionally conservative investor. The investor who goes by the old rules today has a hard time of it and will continue to have a hard time of it. A determined effort has to be made to change existing rules which hamper flexibility and adaptability in a yo-yo world.

We need to question all the old mores, the old rules, the old customs. We need to consider whether they are suitable in a highly inflationary, changeable world. Not only are the mores to be questioned but, even more important, we need to re-examine and re-evaluate investment objectives. The irony today is that the traditionally prudent man may actually be imprudent.

Analyzing Management's Long-Term Potential

WILLIAM R. HAMBRECHT
Senior Partner, Hambrecht & Quist

My investment philosophy is based on the premise that you should not think of an investment in terms of a number that sells at a multiple of other numbers. You should look at an investment as buying a piece of a business. If you do this, short-term earnings results have very little meaning; it forces you to judge management on whether it is running the business for maximum short-term results or whether it truly is trying to build a long-term business.

Unfortunately, our system tends to put great pressure on management to show short-term results. Since Wall Street demands ever-improving earnings, many times management will seriously compromise its long-term position in its industry by showing good profitability at the expense of the product development or personnel development or any other area that is really important to the long-term health of the company.

I think the reason I have enjoyed venture capital investing so much is that I still think one can make a common-sense decision as to whether somebody is really trying to build a business. You can spend time with the management, get a strong feel for its philosophy, and can start to get a feel for the decision processes that work within the company. I find when companies get too big, I lose that feel and have to rely on pure financial analysis.

The best managers break down their business into manageable parts that make sense as an individual business. This keeps a sense of accountability working throughout the business and a sense of control that sometimes gets lost in the larger, multidivisional companies.

It's interesting to look back at some of the successful and unsuccessful investments we've made. It fascinates me how, with the wisdom of hindsight, we can see some of the crucial decisions that were made that in effect made or broke a company. Almost without fail, the most unsuccessful businesses made decisions based on short-term circumstances, and the people who had the courage and the patience to make the long-term decisions built the really successful businesses.

If You Wouldn't Want to Own the Business, Don't Buy the Stock

LUCIEN O. HOOPER
Vice President, Thomson McKinnon Securities, Inc.

On the basis of 66 years' experience of writing about investments, I am impatient with all "systems" designed to beat the market as well as with the technical approach. It is best to regard common stocks as exactly what they are: fractions of ownership in a business. If you don't want to own the business, don't buy the stock. At this time, with inflation likely to continue over the years, natural resource issues should be in high favor. This also is a time to buy good management. Management's tasks in the next decade will be unusually difficult. Because of management traditions, some companies have strong bloodlines. Others don't.

I have learned that most of my "smart ideas" about the stock market as a whole have been worthless. And time spent trying to guess what the market will do has been at least 90 percent wasted. You don't buy "the market." You buy individual stocks. Even if you knew the tops and bottoms of the stock market, you could not take advantage of such intelligence to more than a small extent.

My success in my own affairs has been based on accumulation of good things, not trading. I try to sell my stocks that go down and keep my stocks that go up. I try to reinvest all my dividends. I try to put a little more money in stocks regularly, in good times and in bad. With me, a wide diversification of risks pays. Others do better when they concentrate. I judge results by five-year cycles, not by six months or a year.

I'm prejudiced in favor of higher-priced stocks. I have found that stocks selling at $50 or $100 usually are more profitable investments than those that sell at $5 or $10.

My ideal, of course, is better than my performance. I make mistakes, but I try to correct them in such a way as to share them with Uncle Sam. At the same time, I try to keep Uncle Sam from sharing too liberally in my profits.

Concentration, Patience, and Consistency

ROBERT B. MENSCHEL

Partner, Goldman, Sachs & Co.

Over the years, I have watched many styles of investing, running the gamut from arbitrage, to option trading, to growth stock investing. An essential for investment success is to find the *single area* you understand best and feel most comfortable with, stick with it and constantly refine it, and leave all other approaches to someone else. From my experience, the simplest way to make money consistently is by investing in growing companies at reasonable multiples, as opposed to speculating. *Consistency* is all important. A $10,000 portfolio that compounds at only 15 percent per year will be worth $40,500 in 10 years and $163,700 in 20 years. That same portfolio, compounding at 20 percent per year will be worth $61,900 in 10 years and $383,400 in 20 years. This type of performance can only be attained by avoiding mistakes. The ability to buy the right growth stocks is important, but the judgment to avoid losses by overpaying for growth is equally necessary.

In selecting growth stocks, it is important to focus on companies that are the leaders in their field, no matter how prosaic or mundane the industry may be. In addition, one should look for above-average management and a high degree of earnings visibility combined with a growth rate of 12–15 percent per year. In order to find these companies, it is important to anticipate and recognize trends, constantly looking for companies that satisfy consumer needs, whether they be greeting card companies, toy retailers, children's shoe companies, or in the home-improvement field. Sustainable earnings growth is usually found where the product is priced under $10 and where there is a strong brand position and above-average product distribution.

Successful investing is really not that difficult but most investors tend to complicate it by lacking patience or being overly concerned with the stock they missed rather than focusing on what they own.

Over periods of time the stock market usually moves back and forth between overvaluation and undervaluation but when one combines the purchase of stock in companies with a low multiple and growth of 12–15 percent per year with some patience, one can look for substantial rewards.

Don't Be Afraid to Take a Loss

GEORGE S. JOHNSTON

President, Scudder, Stevens & Clark

An important ingredient of net gain is loss. If you want to earn profits over a period of time, you must expect some losses along the way. If you over-focus on the loss, or hesitate to take it when you should, you reduce your chances of net gain. If you are highly sensitive about losses, you should assess yourself as to whether you are truly a long-term investor and can take the risk that opportunity entails.

When you invest, you buy only the future; someone already owns the past. Too often, investors project the past into the future and sometimes fall in love with securities where the fundamentals have truly changed, or they have become too high-priced even though they remain sound on a fundamental basis. The discipline of looking to the future encompasses not only an analysis of what the future may hold in terms of basic developments, growth, and change; it starts most importantly with present market price. It is price that is the key determinant of investment success, the price at which you buy and also the price at which you sell—and the future should be viewed from this perspective.

Cutting Losses and Letting Profits Ride

BERNARD J. LASKER

*Senior Partner, Lasker, Stone & Stern,
and former Chairman, New York Stock Exchange*

The most important thing I've learned in 58 years on Wall Street is to reverse human nature when a stock I have bought goes down. Human nature is to hope that things will work out when they start to go wrong. I have learned to fear that things will get worse rather than better when they start going wrong. In other words, when I buy a stock and it starts to go down, I fear that it will go down even more, rather than hope it will come back to where it was when I bought it.

Conversely, when I buy a stock and it goes up, I again reverse human nature. Most people feel that when they have a quick profit, they better take it before they lose it. But when I have a profit, I let it ride, hoping that it will get bigger rather than fearing that it will go back down.

How Swiss Bankers Invest Internationally

HANS J. BAER
Chairman, The Julius Baer Group, Zurich

It is more important to protect invested capital than to aim for unrealistic and unsustainable short-term gains.

It is essential to spread political and economic risks by investing internationally. Investments should be made only in politically stable countries with a democratically elected government and an economic policy that allows a prosperous free enterprise system. The country should also have an immaculate long-term record of servicing and repaying its internal debts. Within these guidelines, North America, Western Europe (excluding most Mediterranean countries), Japan, and Australia are strongly preferred. In addition, a number of supranational organizations with a very strong backing from the most developed industrial countries in the Free World (e.g., World Bank, Inter-American Development Bank, European Investment Bank) are excellent vehicles for bond investments.

In spite of the efforts made by various governments and central banks to gain better control over short-term currency fluctuations, currency selection will remain one of the most important investment criteria.

The currency should be freely convertible, and there should be no (or very few) restrictions on the free transfer of capital for foreigners and residents of the country. Financial markets should be highly developed and sophisticated. This limits the number of currencies that should be considered for investment to only a few: the U.S. dollar, Swiss franc, West

German mark, Japanese yen, Dutch guilder, and pound sterling. For investments in equities, a small number of additional currencies might be considered, providing that the good prospects for stock investments outweigh the currency risk.

The asset mix (i.e., the proportion of equity investments on the one hand and fixed-interest investments on the other hand) has to be both flexible and actively managed in order to take advantage of changing market conditions.

The return on fixed-interest investments (money market instruments, bonds, convertible bonds) in strong currencies will remain competitive with investments in equities under most circumstances, and generally at a lower risk.

Convertible bonds often are particularly attractive investment instruments for conservative investors who would like to have a piece of the stock market action and at the same time limit the risk of capital losses. If high-quality convertible bonds provide the same or nearly the same yield as straight bonds, which on occasion happens in the secondary market, there is, in fact, hardly an excuse for not using the convertibles.

Where convertibles sell in the aftermarket at virtually the same yield level as straight bonds with compatible maturities, they should be preferred. That's because in an improved stock market environment, the conversion right may well become attractive again. There also is a broad choice of high-quality convertible bonds on international markets that offer interesting currency features. A large number of Japanese corporations, among them many names of international fame, have issued convertible bonds payable in West German marks. These bonds offer the attraction of one of the strongest currencies combined with a conversion feature into stocks traded on the most dynamic of the major stock markets. Similarly, there are bonds denominated in Swiss francs or U.S. dollars that are convertible into Japanese equities, and even a few U.S. corporations have issued convertible bonds in foreign currencies, such as West German marks or Swiss francs.

For equity investments, choose those countries with a favorable economic and political climate and concentrate on those industries that offer above-average growth potential.

The tax system should allow adequate rates of depreciation and encourage capital formation. Labor, if well organized, should appreciate the free enterprise system and should not hamper technical progress by rigid work rules. The educational system of the country should have a high (and increasing) standard, and the government should encourage or support research in key areas of scientific and technical development.

Besides North America, Japan, Australia, and a number of countries in Western Europe such as West Germany, Great Britain, France, the Netherlands, and Switzerland, there are other areas where stock investments should be considered. A number of Far Eastern countries are showing fast technical/industrial progress and may well develop into interesting investment areas once their financial markets have become more mature. In South Africa, gold mining shares appear to offer good medium- to long-term prospects, but political developments have to be watched very closely.

Ten Rules for Stock Market Failure (Or, How to Lose Money Without Really Trying)

MARK J. APPLEMAN
Publisher, The Corporate Shareholder

1. Try to strike it rich quickly.

2. Aim at buying at the lowest and selling at the highest price.

3. Follow tips and impulses in your trading.

4. Decide against building a balanced portfolio because you have only a small amount to invest.

5. Fail to define your investment goals.

6. Become enamored by high-performance stocks without bothering to do any investigation.

7. Attempt to use esoteric market tools (puts and calls, shorting, etc.) without using extreme caution.

8. Neglect to take into account both fundamental and technical factors before buying a stock.

9. Buy a stock on the basis of its past performance rather than on its future potential.

10. Fail to review your investments on a regular basis.

It's Money that Makes the Market Go Round

STEFAN ABRAMS
Chairman, Investment Policy Committee, Oppenheimer & Co.

Bull markets come and go. The strongest influence is money. It is axiomatic that all financial assets float on a sea of liquidity which rises and falls over the course of an economic cycle. Stocks, bonds, and even commodities require fuel to propel them higher, and when that fuel—in the form of excess liquidity—is missing, these instruments have no place to go but down. The history of stock market fluctuations is a study of the ebb and flow of residual liquidity.

There are several ways to measure the amount of liquidity in the financial system to push the prices of financial assets higher. We call these liquidity proxies. The idea behind these proxies is to measure marginal changes in the amount of money being created by the Federal Reserve Board versus the amount of money being pre-empted by the commercial and industrial transactions for the purchase of goods and services.

If a customer borrows $10,000 from a bank to purchase an automobile, the bank may get the funds for the customer from either excess reserves, the sale of a Treasury bill, or a bid for someone to buy a certificate of deposit. In the first instance, the excess reserves are deployed with only a slight impact on the liquidity proxy, whereas in the second and third cases the effect is more direct and tends to reduce available liquidity and to raise interest rates. Admittedly, the impact of a single transaction of this nature is infinitessimal, but when millions of such transactions take place more or less in tandem, the effect is quite significant.

In order to tell whether the general environment is conducive to higher prices for stocks and bonds one should look at the rate of growth of money supply (M1) over the past one-, three-, six-, and twelve-month periods. This growth rate should then be compared with the rate of growth of total credit demands from government, business, and household borrowers. If there has been an excess of money created over the past three to twelve months, it will probably already be manifest in rising stock and bond markets. If there has been a shortage for three months or more, it is probable that interest rates will already be higher and stocks and bonds lower. The financial markets tend to respond to shifts in available liquidity with only a short time lag of anywhere from one to three months. The economy itself responds to these changes with a lag of about six months, although in recent years the lags have tended to contract.

Another indication of available liquidity can be obtained by viewing the shape of the yield curve, which is a graphical depiction of yields for securities of the same quality but having maturities varying from overnight to 30 or 40 years. For example, if the yield on three-month Treasury bills is substantially above the yield on long-term Treasury bonds having a maturity of from 10 to 30 years, then it is likely that the financial system is being starved for liquidity. People are selling financial assets to pay for goods and services. They may well be engaged in distress borrowing to pay for the carrying of unwanted inventories or slow-paying receivables. This is hardly an environment in which stocks and bonds can do well.

On the other hand, once the Federal Reserve Board believes that a period of tight money has gone far enough, it is forced (usually by mounting bankruptcies) to relax its grip on money supply and accelerate its growth. Then, the steeply inverted yield curve changes configuration very quickly. Within a month or two, short-term interest rates will plunge to a level far below long-term rates as the Federal Reserve Board cranks up money supply growth again, flooding the system with liquidity just at the time when commercial transactions are reaching a low point, i.e., the trough of a recession. It is during this reliquification period, which usually lasts anywhere from six to twelve months, that the sharpest and most broadly based rallies in stock and bond prices take place.

Beyond this period, the economy will most likely have begun to recover, and the resulting increase in activity by consumers and businesses, together with the financing requirements of government at all levels, will require more liquidity for everyday transactions. Unless the Federal Reserve were to further accelerate its printing of money to a highly inflationary level, therefore, there will be less money available for propelling financial assets higher. Accordingly, the remainder of the stock market cycle will be less broadly based, and the advance will be less sharp and punctuated with more periods of correction. Throughout this entire bull market cycle, which will end when credit demands push short-term interest rates above long-term rates once again, it is of paramount importance that investors know at what stage they are at, so as not to buy or sell indiscriminately.

The irony is that although the stock market is typically referred to as a discounting mechanism, what I have been discussing is really a residual effect. Stocks move up ahead of corporate profit growth (i.e., recovery) merely because the greatest degree of available liquidity occurs in the late stages of a recession when the Fed is trying to get the economy's motor started up again and is flooding the system with money.

Of course, none of this is worth much to an investor unless he has specific stocks to buy. In that regard, it may be useful to think of the stock market as one enormous arbitrage, in the course of which undervalued issues are constantly moving higher relative to the average of all issues, while overvalued issues are stalling out or even declining. Pockets of undervaluation occur in many areas and in many forms. The key things to watch for are companies that have:

• A strong industrial profile, particularly with respect to market share unit growth and return on equity;

- A strong financial profile, particularly unit and revenue growth;

- A return on both assets and equity; and

- A positive relationship between their stock market valuation and an appropriate benchmark, such as either other companies in the same industry or a broad market average, such as the Standard & Poor's 500.

The undervaluation may be a function of rapidly recovering profits, newly emerging growth of earnings, corporate restructuring by spin-off or disposal of losing divisions, or by equity shrinkage through a stock repurchase. In all cases, companies that are generating excess cash are more interesting than those whose cash generation is modest or insufficient to financial growth. Of course, a company investing heavily for the future may not yet have reached that point. Accordingly, the investor will have to count on management's ability to succeed and be patient enough to wait for the results.

The market may or may not agree and will act accordingly until the results are in. When rising liquidity is lifting the whole level of equity values, a trained monkey throwing darts at the stock tables can achieve good returns, especially in the buying stampedes that have come to characterize today's heavily institutionalized and fiercely competitive markets. The route to consistently superior results, however, lies in identifying truly undervalued equities in the many forms these take.

Value can be found in a stream of annual earnings-per-share increases, although these are not always predictable and usually do not last for many years. Furthermore, by the time a company has put together a string of impressive earnings gains the premium valuation of its shares usually reflects the record, and there is no longer a compelling undervaluation.

At the opposite end of the spectrum, one can often find companies whose earnings patterns have been erratic, declining, or even negative, but where new management or new strategies are in place to reverse the company's fortunes. Typically, these shares have been abandoned by investors and are selling at depressed valuations, particularly relative to future earning power. Often, they are below stated book value and even further below the true market value of the company's assets. Even if a rehabilitation plan is unsuccessful, the near-term risk in the share price is likely to be small, since the market rarely pays up in advance for an industrial turnaround, the way it usually does for a growth company. If the shares can be purchased below book value just as return on equity (profits divided by book value) is beginning to recover, the investors's return will be even higher than the company's own return on investment. In time, the improved profitability will usually result in a substantial upward valuation of the shares to a new equilibrium compared with the overall market.

Yet another related concept of value that has come into vogue in recent years looks at companies as if they were parcels of income-producing real estate. Many companies in relatively prosaic businesses earning satisfactory but unspectacular returns, or capable of same if rehabilitated, can be attractive purchases. Merely because the stock market is unimpressed and values the shares cheaply, they become attractive leveraged buyouts either by their own management teams or by another corporation for whom the returns are still attractive even at a premium takeover price. A large amount of debt may be required to effect the transaction, but if the cash flow from the business is table, it can often amortize this debt over a relatively short time frame, paying off the mortgage so to speak, and leaving the new owner with a valuable equity. All of this is similar to the redemption of a home mortgage by the owner out of the proceeds of his income. Even if the transaction is only a partial one, as the company buys back a significant percentage of its own stock, the rewards for the remaining shareholders can be quite worthwhile.

Wherever value is found, however, the hallmarks of deep undervaluation include a stock selling at a modest multiple of earnings, cash flow, or book value. In terms of earnings these may be actual or prospective if some rehabilitation is presumed to be taking place. The degree of free cash flow over and above the amount required to be reinvested to sustain the current size and profitability of the business, so-called undedicated cash flow, measured on a pretax basis, gives an approximation of the funds available to service the debt which might be incurred in a leveraged buyout or takeover. The value of a company relative to its assets, even those not stated on the balance sheet, is equally important. Some investor or businessman will be willing to pay market value for mineral holdings or other real estate, an overfunded pension plan, or even a tax loss carryforward, just to name a few.

In a dynamic sense, as long as any company is maintaining its market share in an industry which is showing overall unit growth and earning a true cash flow, the shares will eventually be valued in line with the degree to which its return on equity exceeds or falls below that achieved by corporations generally. The potential risk or reward, therefore, can be approximated by comparing the relative price/book value ratio of the individual stock to its relative return on equity using the values for a broad market average as reference points. If the relative valuation (price/book value) is far below the relative profitability (return on equity) there is an opportunity for an upward revaluation of the stock. The opposite condition measures potential risk, although it should be noted that stocks which earn a premium return on equity relative to the market usually command a premium valuation. Those which earn a chronically sub-par return rarely close the gap.

PART THREE

MEETING THE INSTITUTIONAL CHALLENGE

The Institutional Secret Behind the Rise in Stock Prices

DONALD I. TROTT

*Director of Research,
Mabon, Nubent & Co.*

While the textbooks leave the impression that the big institutional investors—a typical bank trust department or an insurance company investment committee—are somewhat staid and harmonious groups, which dutifully ponder such profound issues as the health and direction of the domestic economy and the implications of world developments, the reality is that more primitive behavioral characteristics are at work. These may be summed up as a drive toward power. Most investment committees are made up of two distinct cliques: a fixed-income-oriented group and an equity-oriented group. The members of each of these cliques are allied by a common job-related self-interest. On either a conscious or at the least subliminal basis, each tends to view the other in a somewhat adversarial manner. These factions are continually vying for control and relative dominance of influence within the overall committee.

A distinct pattern has emerged with respect to the recurring shifts in control of these committees and the resultant impact on the equities market. These patterns generally unfold on a fairly universal basis and within a somewhat set time frame, usually four to six years. When such a shift occurs, it may become the single most important influence on stock prices over the ensuing several years.

To illustrate this point, let's turn the clock back to the late 1960s. At that time, the investment decision-making committees of most major institutions came to be dominated by its equity-oriented component. As a result, those institutions virtually simultaneously sought to increase the percentage of their investment portfolios allocated to equities. Furthermore, since nearly all were caught up in the relative performance game (which is characterized by each portfolio manager attempting to outperform the competition each and every quarter), most tended to focus on the same universe of stocks—those that were acting the best—in this instance, America's fastest-growing premier companies, the so-called nifty-fifty, which were accumulated under a "buy and hold" philosophy.

Since most institutions were handling increasingly larger pools of money and allocating a continually increasing percentage of these resources (for the most part) to the same stocks, the typical institutional portfolio achieved highly enviable gains over the next several years. But this superior performance was largely self-fulfilling. Between 1968 and 1972, average institutional equity exposure rose from about 54 percent to a whopping 76 percent. As a result, stock prices had nowhere to go but up! Price/earnings ratio yardsticks kept on advancing, despite a steady supply of new equity financings. And the institutions responded with enthusiasm to suggestions from their clients that their managed portfolios be heavily oriented toward stocks.

Equity Domination

Paradoxically, the very same corporate treasurers who, while wearing their pension fund administrative hats, were urging investment managers to increase overall equity exposure watched in near-disbelief as the shares of their own corporations were bid up to what they recognized to be unrealistic levels. They responded with a steady flow of new equity financings to exploit the seemingly insatiable institutional appetite for common stocks, which they themselves were helping to fuel.

The state of the economy, the Vietnam war, the devaluation of the dollar, and rioting in the streets counted for naught. Institutional committees had come to be dominated by stock-oriented decisioin makers, and so equity prices moved upward. It was as simple as that.

Buoyed by their success, the control of equity-oriented members of the typical committee continued to increase. Little attention was being paid to the fixed-income-oriented cointingent who continued to urge that a greater percentage of funds be allocated to the bond market. While they were correct in their view that equity prices had been driven to excessive levels, no one heeded their alarm. They had cried "Wolf!" too many times throughout the prior stock market surge.

In January 1973, the stock market peaked. With three-quarters of all institutional dollars already dedicated to common stocks, there were insufficient incremental funds available to continue to support the already lofty level of equity prices. The stock market had nowhere to go but down! While the typical institution gradually began to decrease the percentage of its assets invested in common stocks, overall they remained heavily committed to equities and generally turned in exceedingly poor performances over the next several years.

Shift in Control

As a result, in the mid-1970s, their influence waned; control began to shift back to the fixed-income-oriented investment managers. Funds began to flow out of equities and into bonds. At first, this strategy proved rewarding. As fixed-income investments provided superior performance to equities, the dominance and influence of fixed-income-oriented committee members continued to increase, and in a few years surpassed that of their equity-oriented counterparts. Bonds were going up and equities were going down. They had to. It was self-fulfilling because nearly all committees were undergoing similar transitions. Customers cried out for a greater percentage of their assets to be dedicated to bonds, and the multiple yardsticks being applied to common stocks began to recede. Institutions became heavy sellers of common stocks, with the proceeds being reinvested in bonds.

This trend continued to accelerate despite the fact that the returns bonds were then providing were below the ongoing rates of inflation then in effect, thereby virtually assuring a negative "real return."

As irrational and masochistic as it may sound, the overriding determinant of this policy was simply that control of institutional investment committees had passed back into the hands of their debt-oriented factions. During the second half of the 1970s, reality eventually caught up with the bond market. The shift in asset allocation toward bonds began to slow as it neared completion, thereby reducing ongoing demand for fixed-income securities. Meanwhile, the supply of new debt offerings continued to swell, reflecting increasing recognition by corporate America that debt financing had become intrinsically cheap. At the same time, however, they remained supportive of the fixed-income orientation of the managers of their pension funds. After all, they had made money for a few years in bonds, while the equity market had been in the doldrums. Moreover, their actuarial consultants, utilizing assumptions that had already been obsolesced, assured them that all of their pension funding problems would be solved by a heavy bond weighting in their portfolios.

Not surprisingly, the bond market collapsed; there was no longer sufficient pent-up institutional buying power to support a self-fulfilling advance in bond prices. By the end of 1979, the equity proportion of the typical institutional portfolio had been reduced to 53 percent, compared with 76 percent seven years before.

The process then began to reverse itself. After several years, during which equity investments had outperformed fixed-income securities, the power within most major institutional investment committees began to shift back again to those oriented toward equities. Between mid-1979 and mid-1980, the process was completed, with most investment decision-making bodies once again firmly in control of their equity-oriented members.

Stocks Move Up

It is for this reason more than any other that equity prices surged dramatically throughout most of 1980. The impact of this phenomenon completely dwarfed the impact of rising interest rates, the lack of public enthusiasm for either of the presidential candidates, the recession, continued high levels of inflation, and all of the other fundamental considerations that many assumed to be the more relevant determinants of the trend of common stock prices. Investors had become disenchanted with the bond market, had urged their money managers to place greater emphasis on equities; and the institutional community had responded. The equity-oriented money manager was back in control, and so equity prices moved up.

During 1980, the typical institution increased the percentage of its steadily growing pool of assets allocated to equities from 53 percent to 58 percent. No wonder equity prices advanced! Once again price/earnings ratio yardsticks began to expand. And, because the stock market had performed well during 1980, customer support for equity investment increased too. The power and committee dominance of the more equity-oriented institutional managers grew as well.

As a result, equity exposure of the typical institutionally managed portfolio continued to expand, advancing to about 62 percent during the first quarter of 1981. Given the recent reascendance of the equity-oriented committee member, there was little doubt that the entire process would once again repeat itself, and indeed it did.

Between March 1981 and March 1982, equity exposure of professionally managed balance funds began to recede, giving a clear-cut interim sell signal by the summer of 1981 as the trend became apparent. By the end of the first quarter of 1982, however, equity exposure had decreased to 51½ percent from 62 percent just twelve months earlier. This represented the lowest level of equity exposure in more than a decade, as well as the largest twelve-month cutback ever. Yet, equity-oriented managers remained in control, with most of the liquidation representing either a shift into bonds as a trading vehicle or the build-up of cash reserves, rather than any enduring commitment to fixed-income securities. Hence, the stage was set for one of the biggest market rallies in history, which, indeed, commenced in August 1983.

By the latter part of 1983, equity exposure of the institutional community had climbed to about 66 percent. Institutional equity exposure will most likely advance to in excess of 70 percent before the impact of the current round of equity dominance of institutional investment committees has been completed, and stock prices will, accordingly, advance as well. This will occur regardless of more conventional fundamental considerations; it will occur because of the shift in power that has taken place within most major institutional committees.

Moreover, price/earnings ratio yardsticks will continue to expand. The general course of the market is dictated by considerations of supply and demand for equities, not by the state of the economy, international developments, or other generally accepted factors. Supply and demand, in turn, are most significantly influenced by the continuous cycle of shift of relative influence among the fixed-income-minded and equity-oriented components of the investment committees of the most powerful institutional investors. Understand where we are at any point in time within this cycle, and one can predict readily the intermediate-term direction of the equity market.

Institutions Set the Trend for the Stock Market

JEAN M. KIRK
*Vice President,
T. Rowe Price Associates*

Monday mornings are important to most institutional investors. That's when they formulate their short-term tactics. Hard facts are learned, and there seems to be a continuing need to digest the weekend papers. Early Monday, portfolio managers meet to discuss individual investment ideas with their peers and check their buy/sell/hold recommendations with the analysts following those companies. The investment committee wants to know what the firm's economist is forecasting for the future trend. And, more than likely, the market technician is consulted for his reading of the chart patterns for the stocks under consideration.

The recent period has not been an easy time for institutional managers. They are educated in skepticism and disbelief. They want to see all the data they can get. They need a "feedforward" kind of skill, but illumination comes in small doses—never in broad, clear flashes of "group think."

The decision to buy, sell, or hold frequently has to be made on slim knowledge. That's where the "skill" of the portfolio manager comes in. Keep in mind that the analyst's responsibility is to determine the value of the stock. The portfolio manager makes the investment decision within the parameters of the market-related information and the institution's objectives. Of course, there are some huge exceptions to the series of actions or operations. Sometimes the committee consists only of two people. Often the analyst's work comes via a written document rather than in person. But no matter how much data is presented, near-term, on Mondays, the investment professional focuses on the tactics for the week.

Next, the logistical process gets underway. Orders must be documented. Meanwhile, the trading day is passing by. Sometimes we see a pick-up in block trading by institutions late on Mondays, but, more often, the big investor comes into the market on Tuesdays. Even then, institutions will wait for somebody to take the lead before they step out with a batch of orders.

This is not to say that all big money managers are necessarily such an investigative lot, but I'm convinced that the best ones are suspicious about everything. From past experience, they have found this is the system that gives the best performance.

When the market goes up 20 points on Monday, or down five, institutional investors tend to sit back and say, "Well, it's just the retail buyer in the market. What does he know?" They infer, and rightly so, that by Tuesday, the "better informed" institutions will be the dominant influence.

The retail buyer in the equity markets reads the same weekend publications, but he doesn't need a committee to approve his investment decisions. He makes up his own mind. Maybe he hears an idea at a cocktail party Saturday night and decides to put in his order the "first thing" Monday morning. And he does. The retail buyer can normally be noticed in the market at the opening of each day, but that is particularly true on Mondays.

Blue Monday

One often hears the phrase "blue Monday." Examination of the data by Arthur A. Merrill of Chappaqua, New York, an expert on cycles, shows that Monday is truly a "blue" day. His update of information (summer

1984) shows the market rose only 43.6 percent of the time, a highly significant deviation from average. At the same time, Fridays are highly significant in a bullish direction. Street smarts would say that Friday is the day when traders sell—to clear the deck for the weekend. But Merrill finds that Friday has a highly significant bullish pattern.

Figure 2 shows that on Mondays in 1984, 63.5 percent of the trading in

FIGURE 2
Retail and Institutional Activity for Each Day of the Week

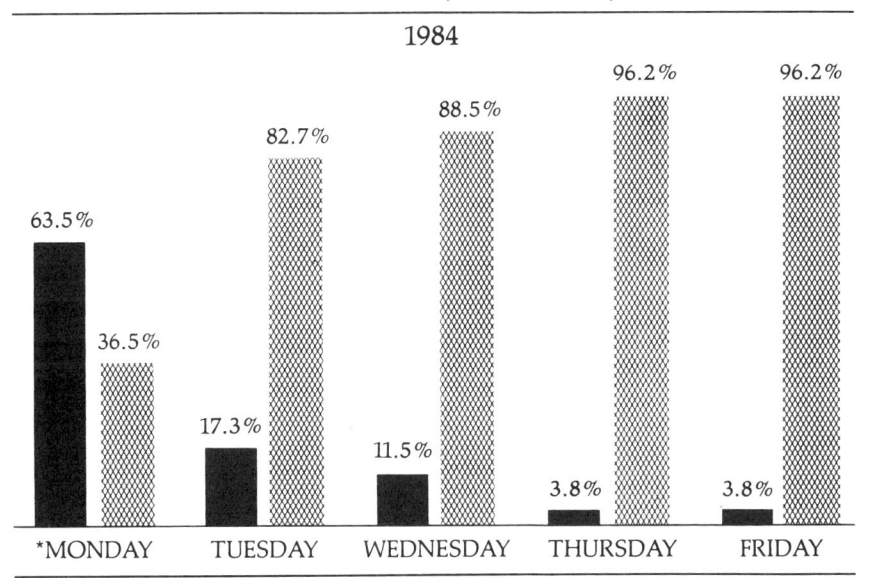

1984

Day	Retail Activity	Institutional Activity
*MONDAY	63.5%	36.5%
TUESDAY	17.3%	82.7%
WEDNESDAY	11.5%	88.5%
THURSDAY	3.8%	96.2%
FRIDAY	3.8%	96.2%

Data is Year-to-Date December 31, 1984
*Monday or the First Day of the Week

■ = Retail Activity   ▨ = Institutional Activity

(Source: Salomon Brothers Inc.)

the market was done by the retail buyer, while on all other days the institutions were dominant. On all the Fridays in the measured period, the institution was dominant.

For how long has this pattern existed? Merrill broke the period into two eight-year periods and adjusted to take care of average bearishness or bullishness in the two periods. 'The conclusion was evident. Monday was blue in both periods; Friday was, on average, enthusiastic in both periods."

Laszlo Birinyi, Jr., of Salomon Brothers, has also noted that the lowest block activity of the week often occurs on Monday, showing the absence of institutions on that day. On the other hand, Fridays tend to have the heaviest institutional trading. Institutional investors "fiddle around" on Mondays, jump into high gear on Tuesdays, become progressively more interested and involved throughout the week.

So, in Figure 3 which represents trading patterns in 1984, there were forty-four Mondays where institutional activity was in the 40 percent

FIGURE 3
Institutional Activity: Breakdown by Day of the Week
Data Covers Through December 31, 1984

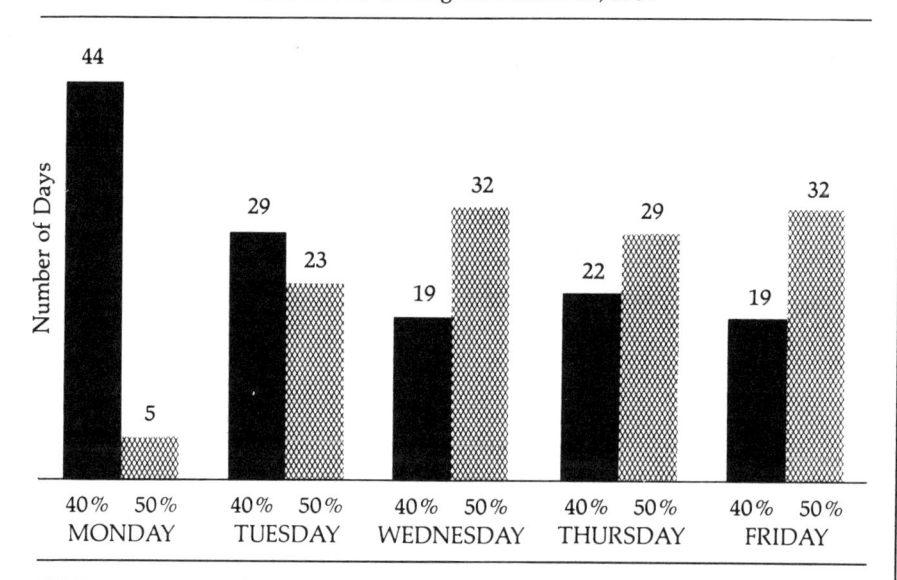

	40%	50%
MONDAY	44	5
TUESDAY	29	23
WEDNESDAY	19	32
THURSDAY	22	29
FRIDAY	19	32

■ = Institutional Activity 40% range
▩ = Institutional Activity 50% range

(Source: Salomon Brothers Inc.)

range and only five Mondays where it was 50 percent or greater. If you take a look at the rest of the week, there are 89 days of institutional activity—around 40 percent and 116 days of 50 percent or better. The data in Figure 4 shows that there is definitely a tendency for institutions to have less activity on Mondays. In fact, in 1984, 63.5 percent of the time Mon-

FIGURE 4
A Historical Look at How Monday Is the Lightest Day of the Week for Block Activity

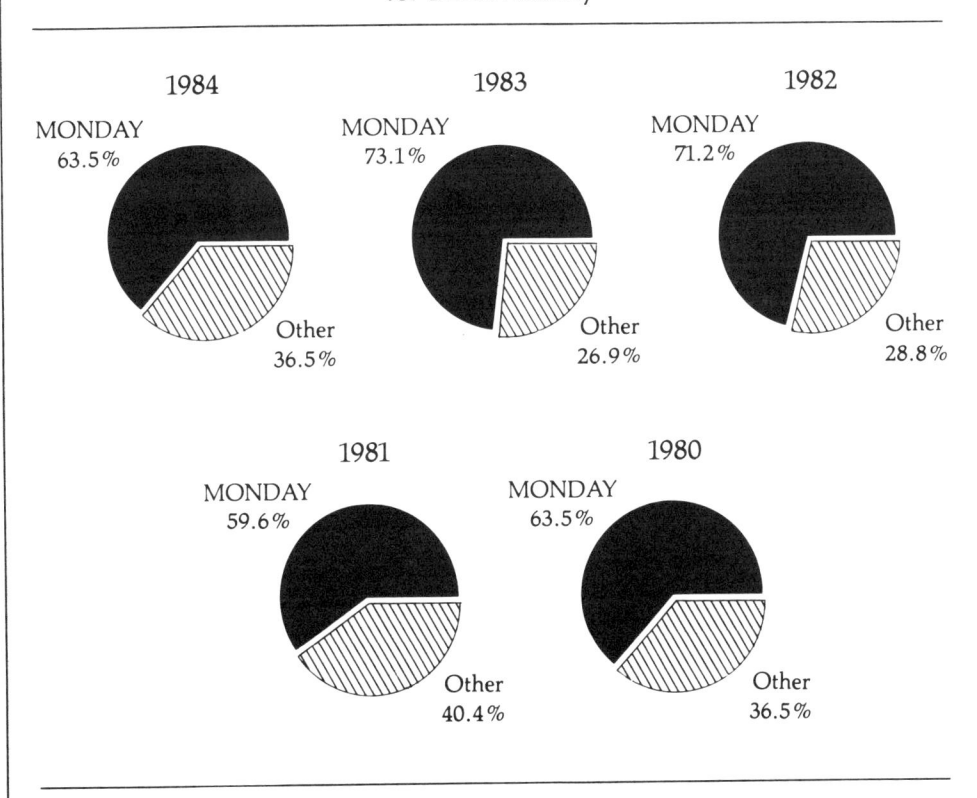

1984
MONDAY 63.5%
Other 36.5%

1983
MONDAY 73.1%
Other 26.9%

1982
MONDAY 71.2%
Other 28.8%

1981
MONDAY 59.6%
Other 40.4%

1980
MONDAY 63.5%
Other 36.5%

■ = Mondays (or First Day of the Week)
\\\\\\ = Other Days of the Week

(Source: Salomon Brothers Inc?)

day was the least active day of the week, and that percentage was even greater in 1983 and 1982.

Institutional Trading

In a public transactions study by the New York Stock Exchange (NYSE), through the fourth quarter of 1980, the distribution of volume on the exchange among members, individuals, and institutions shows that individuals were responsible for 35 percent of the shares traded on the NYSE and institutions accounted for 65 percent.

A commonly quoted number is the dollar volume, and it is slightly different. In dollars, individuals were responsible for 28 percent of public volume and institutions accounted for 72 percent. (Members trades were eliminated to discuss what is called "public volume.")

We can conclude that the investment business is in the process of becoming more institutionally dominated than ever before. Even though individuals still own two-thirds of all the common stock in this country, in terms of trading activity, institutions account for about three-quarters of a given day's activity and the public accounts for one-quarter.

Nobody has really figured out how to measure John Q. Public's stock market performance. But Merrill Lynch's big data base shows that cash accounts usually buy more and more as the market averages go down, so they wind up doing the heaviest buying—or having the highest buy-sell ratio—around the month of an important market bottom. The public might start buying too soon, but as the market declines more and more, its ratio of buying to selling goes up.

Therefore, at the point where the market has stopped going down the public is consistently doing the heaviest buying. The only time where there was a seemingly glaring quirk in that figure was in 1982, when retail cash account customers bought in the first month or two of 1982 but then turned back to selling. At the bottom in July-August 1982, they were actually heavy sellers. That was the first time where individual investors were not heavy buyers at what was considered a market bottom. But even that exception needs some explanation. Although the market averages didn't make their lows until early August 1982, many stocks had made their lows in late 1981 or early 1982. In many respects, a lot of stocks were already starting to go up—or at least had stopped going down. So these retail buyers, who tend to buy weakness, were not enticed to buy more and more because their stocks were no longer going down. John Q. Public's ratio, in this one instance, swung back to the sell side.

A Solomon Brothers study shows that for the first three months of 1984 individuals, not institutions, were bailing out of the stock market. By Laszlo Birinyi's calculations, retail customers withdrew $28.6 billion from the market during the period while institutions increased their investment by $11.3 billion. "It's not so much that the institutions were more bullish, it's just that many of them have cash coming in all the time that they have to put to work in something," he points out.

Back in 1971, when White House Chief of Staff and former Treasury Secretary Donald T. Regan was the head of Merrill Lynch, he noted that the retail buyer was really better on a value basis because he was early. That is to say, the retail buyer tends to buy or sell on a yield basis. When short-term interest rates were coming down, that frequently prompted a more aggressive approach toward equities while institutions sometimes became more progressively pessimistic.

Nevertheless, what we really need to understand is that the institutional investor sets the course. And even though individuals may be dominant in the market on Monday and at the beginning of each trading day, we need to wait until we see volume and buying on Tuesday to discern the trend of the market.

How Individual Investors Can Outperform the Giant Institutions

ERIC T. MILLER

*Senior Vice President and
Chief Investment Policy Officer
Donaldson, Lufkin & Jenrette, Inc.*

It is understandable that the giant investment institutions awe many individual investors. The sheer size of their assets, their market power, and the seemingly huge amount of information and knowledge at their disposal can overwhelm the amateur. Some are tempted to find out how and why the investment behemoths made their decisions—and then to emulate them. Although it is important to appreciate their size, market role, and how they operate, it's well to remember that although many of the best and brightest minds in our country are busily occupied managing investment money, only a few have had consistently outstanding records of success.

Does that mean that investment success is too elusive and difficult for the average investor to realize? Absolutely not. The individual investor should recognize that today's institutional investing has many handicaps and impediments that don't apply to him.

There is no reason why the individual investor cannot match and perhaps even exceed the returns achieved by the best institutional managers with less knowledge and much less time. To do so, however, the investor must have considerable understanding and discipline. Our advice is to understand the institution's role and then invest differently from most—that is, be much longer-term in approach, and develop the patience of Job.

Bigger and More Dominant Than Ever

Most people have long appreciated the importance of institutions in the marketplace, but they may have failed to recognize how much their dominance has increased in recent years. For example, block trades of 10,000 shares or more accounted for about 50 percent of daily New York Stock Exchange volume in the first half of 1984, up from 27 percent as recently as 1980, and 5 percent in 1965. The average turnover of equity investment assets of major pension funds was about 65 percent in 1983, up from 20 percent ten years ago. With the growth of pension fund assets at the corporate and public retirement level, institutions probably have been accounting for 75–80 percent of daily trading recently.

With the vast information resources and services available to skilled specialists and generalists earlier and more quickly than ever before, how can the average individual compete? Particularly since the transaction costs are less to the big investor and most are in a non-taxable status.

Different Demands and Different Objectives

The individual investor should understand some things about institutional investors. True, they are a varied group with different shapes, sizes, and investment styles. But the key difference is that they are managing someone else's money—not their own—and their success as a hiree depends increasingly on their performance against the market over a relatively short time.

Their objective is account retention, beating the competition, and generally (but not always) new account growth. Personal financial rewards and peer-group admiration stem from good performance. They intensely wish to survive, to retain their job positions and employability. Quarterly performance is their report card, but they are aware that increasingly the client or the client's advisory consultant is monitoring results, perhaps even weekly.

More and more often, an investment firm is hired for a particular investment style, say as a growth-stock specialist, value investor, or one supposedly expert at market timing. Deviations from that style or below-average performance within that classification prompt questions and, perhaps, the termination of the client relationship. And as they say, "a portfolio manager without an account is no longer a portfolio manager." The mental pressures have therefore been escalating steadily in recent years.

Wild Eruptions and Sharp Declines

The increasing dominance of the institutional investor and the performance pressures have altered market patterns over the last fifteen years. Investment horizons have grown shorter and shorter, and few professional money managers believe that they any longer have the luxury of being long-term investors. It used to be said that bull markets tend to last three times as long as bear markets, and during much of the early and mid stages of advancing markets, the general public was hardly aware of the rising price trends. That came in the later stages.

But that was when markets were dominated by individual investors and bank trust departments. Increasingly, since early in the 1970s, market rises have come in big bursts of volume concentrated in periods of a few months or even weeks, to be followed by longer periods of correction or trading type markets.

Today, because of their size and dominance, institutional investors have become the crowd. By definition, that means that they may determine the primary trend, but that a majority of them will be wrong at major turning points. The institutions are the ones now driving the markets to excess in both violent upmoves and sharp tumbles. Often, those sharp movements may have little relevance to economic activity, but represent shifts in the psychology of the institutions. Professional investors are just as subject to crowd psychology and group thinking as the less experienced and untrained individual. Their attitudes can go to the same extremes of optimism and pessimism as anyone else's.

What Then Is One To Do?

You must first accept the idea that major investors are subject to human foibles at the same time they are burdened with pressures that the individual is relatively free from. Then, you can develop confidence that you can still do well in the marketplace amid the giants. That doesn't mean that the process is easy and that all one has to do is to form logical investment conclusions. H.L. Mencken once said that "there is always an easy solution to every problem—neat, plausible, and wrong."

You should resist, then, the temptation to think conventionally. You should first figure out what the economy is going to do and just invest accordingly. In fact, one of the most frequent errors of institutions right now is to place too much emphasis on top-down thinking, that is, using an economic forecast as the basis for investment strategy and selection.

The individual would be better off adopting a different time horizon than the typical institution, preferably a much longer one, and then use a disciplined approach in the selection of securities. Most should avoid timing the market itself because very few of even the brightest institutional investors are good at it. Best to concentrate on the selection of securities at attractive prices. A security well bought is often well sold. That is, if most securities are bought when they are undervalued, subsequent selling decisions are much easier.

Contrarian Methodologies

A number of disciplined approaches to investing are uncomplicated and have shown consistently above-average results over long periods. They are also approaches that have been well-articulated by some investment leaders. Therefore, they are easily learned by the less experienced. The particular ones that I suggest the average investor consider are the following:

1. The "best businesses approach." The foremost exponent of this methodology is probably Warren Buffett, now an almost legendary figure in the investment profession. The best way to acquaint yourself with Buffett's philosophy is to secure copies of his annual letters to the shareholders of Berkshire Hathaway, available by writing directly to Berkshire Hathaway.

Bill Ruane, head of the Sequoia Fund, has practiced this approach with great success over a long period. Essentially, it involves buying shares in only the best businesses during the infrequent times when they are reasonably priced. Because most businesses and companies are considered not worth owning, seek out only those good ones when there are distress periods in the market created by credit stringency or recession or some seeming crisis. That means being very patient or, as Warren Buffett said, being a good baseball batter who is just waiting up there at the plate, prepared to swing at only the pitch he wants.

2. Low P/E stocks. It has been well demonstrated over long periods of time that those who buy only those stocks with low price/earnings ratios and who hold them until they have achieved popular or average price/earnings multiples consistently do better than average. One of the best spokesmen for this approach is David Dreman, and his book, *The New Contrarian Investment Strategy* (Random House, 1982), is one of the most important investment books written in recent years.

3. The Price-to-Sales Approach. This is a variation on the low-P/E approach of buying out-of-favor stocks and is described in an interesting fashion in Ken Fisher's book *Super Stocks* (Dow Jones Irwin, 1984). Essentially, this approach isolates companies whose market value comprises a low ratio to that of the companies sales or revenues. Often, it leads to companies with virtually no current earnings, but if other essential screens are applied involving balance-sheet strength and financial liquidity, purchase is suggested with the expectation that the holding period will be a long one, from two to five years.

4. Other Variations of Contrarian Investing. Some other ways to avoid the big institutional investors and to profit from their problems include the "long base" approach, or one described in Craig Fecel's book *How to Profit From the Psycle* (Richardson and Snyder, 1984). The long base involves using technical chart analysis as a way of uncovering out-of-favor issues with promise. As described by Ted Warren in his book, *How to Make the Stock Market Make Money for You* (Sherbourn Press, 1965), one searches amid long-term charts for stocks that have languished in long sideways pattern for from four to seven-or-so years but appear to be moving up from those bases. Warren advocated eschewing fundamental analysis altogether and just buying such stocks with the expectation of major upmoves that might take several years.

We think that some fundamental checking is always necessary as Craig Fecel's newer analysis suggests. Fecel's approach attempts to minimize price risk by buying stocks only when they are near ten- or twenty-year lows, but also minimizing business risk by accumulating only seasoned, high-quality companies.

The Psychological Hang-Ups

There is nothing complicated about any of these methods, and analysis suggests that they have stood the tests of time. Each method attempts to minimize risk rather than to maximize gain. Each has succeeded in providing above-average gains. Easy? In a sense, but the real difficulty is in the patience involved where one finds only occasional times when it's appropriate to buy and then one is required to hold on for far longer periods than is fashionable today. So it's apt to be rewarding but for some not terribly exciting. In fact, most of the securities that would be selected would generally be considered to be boring.

For those who feel compelled to be more involved in the mainstream and to be more active, we suggest this. Take a small part of your investment assets, say 10 percent to 20 percent and invest, if you will, in a more venturesome, aggressive fashion. But for the bulk of your money that is committed to common stocks, adopt one or a combination of the methodologies described. After a period of years, you might well merit the envy and admiration of many institutional investors.

Principles of Investing for Big Pension Funds Can Also Apply to Small Investors

ARTHUR WILLIAMS III
Vice President, Pension Fund Investments
Merrill Lynch, Inc.

Many investors dealing only with their own relatively small portfolios are somewhat intimidated by the large amounts of money—sometimes reaching billions of dollars—in large institutional portfolios. The feeling may be that "I don't stand a chance against the big guys." However, this need not be the case. While the mechanics of investing huge sums may be different, the principles are the same regardless of the amount of money involved. These principles can be summarized as follows:

1. Design your investment program for your own particular needs. Consider your age, the number of years you expect to work, the amount of money you have available (after putting aside a contingency fund for emergencies), and your (and your spouse's) willingness to take risk. Don't take advice blindly from your neighbors or friends. Even if they are experienced investors, their requirements may be different than yours.

2. Diversify your investments. One of the cardinal rules of investing is "Don't put all of your eggs in one basket, since, if you drop that basket, you'll have nothing left but one omelet." Consider the meaning of diversification—owning assets which behave differently and which have different risk characteristics. The idea is to recognize that you must give up the high potential for gain which comes from owning a single "hot" investment in order to avoid the potential for a large loss if your one hot idea turns cold.

3. Build a portfolio starting with the most conservative assets. Start with savings, cash reserves, and bonds. Then, expand into stocks and real estate.

4. Take advantage of tax benefits which the government provides to encourage saving. An individual retirement plan, is a good example. In your IRA, lean toward high income bonds rather than stocks. A capital gain in stocks is partly wasted in a tax-sheltered IRA since you pay ordinary income tax rates on all distributions when you retire.

5. Take a long-term view. Markets rise and fall. If you stick to quality and diversify your holdings, you'll avoid the worst mistake an investor can make—panicking in or out of the market at the wrong time.

6. Keep value and common sense in mind at all times. If you can't understand the investment or if you can't see the benefits to you, pass it up. In the long run, value will win out. If you look for value, rather than chasing what is in vogue, you will rarely make the huge blunder which is financially and psychologically damaging—and you will position yourself for sound investment returns.

PART FOUR

STOCK MARKET SECRETS

Analyzing Yourself as an Investor

If a man have only one kind of sense, let him have common sense. If he has that and uncommon sense too, he is not far from genius.
—HENRY WARD BEECHER

Investing is an imperfect science. If it weren't, there would be no buying and trading, because we'd all be holding the right stocks at the right time. Since we don't, we need all the help we can get. Some people are convinced that following a specific stock market system will lead them to riches. As for me, I've never found a system that satisfied me. I'm particularly skeptical of the get-rich-quick schemes that spring up with heavy promotion every so often. I don't know of any such method that actually works. And, if one did exist, I don't know of anyone who would stop raking in his winnings long enough to bother putting it between hard covers or in an envelope or, worse yet, in a high-pressure telephone call.

What I would urge you to do is develop a common sense approach to investing. First, understand what the pitfalls are and how to avoid them, keeping in mind that some of the most common and most difficult to overcome are hidden in your own psyche. Then, try to come up with some guidelines that fit your own financial means, psychology, and investment goals and can be adapted to changing stock market climates. Remember, on Wall Street there is no single set of principles for all seasons. Nothing is as certain as change.

Next, be honest with yourself. You would be surprised how many people are not; they make investment decisions in haste, on whim, or as a result of supposedly hot tips and then justify them with some other reasons. If you fool yourself, you're the only victim. In this regard, I like to recall that when John D. Rockefeller, Sr., once was asked to put in a few words the reasons for the success of Standard Oil, he thought for a moment and then answered: "We never deceived ourselves."

Most important, try to develop the ability to sell. It's a common failing to regard the stocks we own as "ours" and become excessively protective about them. If they're down in price from where we bought them, we wait, hoping they will get back into the plus column (thus vindicating our original judgment). If they're ahead, we hold them for still greater gains (thus indicating that we're increasingly smarter). As a result, we fail to accept new information that changes the perceptions that led to the original investment decision. That's not very surprising. People are instinctively resistant to change, too willing to base future expectations on the continuation of the status quo. Don't get locked into a specific thesis and disregard contrary data that comes your way. It's always a good idea when making an investment decision to sketch out in your mind the things that can go wrong. That will both help you make a balanced decision and alert you to what negative signs to watch for.

And if there's one piece of advice that I'm going to keep emphasizing in this book, it's this: Don't insist on running with the crowd. The biggest investment opportunities often lie in going against the conventional wisdom. There's an irrational tendency to invest heavily in whatever is in fashion. Going with the crowd is a dangerous habit. In the long run, the crowd usually loses, although it can feel very comfortable to be part of it.

"Orthodoxy, particularly when it is embellished by constant repetition, is almost always reassuring to the person who hears it," says Peter Bernstein, economist, author, and money manager in his book, *Economist on Wall Street*. "When one deals constantly with the unknown and when every decision means taking another risk, the warm familiarity of what one has heard before (even if it is wrong) provides an urgently needed sense of security. The unknown is frightening enough; why exacerbate matters by listening to unfamiliar and radical ideas that someone else may put forth?"

"But the hard truth," Bernstein adds, "is that investment success comes most generously to those who are able to swim upstream; majority opinion is already reflected in the current level of security prices."

H.L. Mencken, although he wasn't referring to stock market behavior, had a somewhat similar view when he described the typical American as *Homo Boobus:* "In all his miscellaneous reactions to ideas, he embraces invariably those that are the simplest, the least unfamiliar, the most comfortable—those that fit in most readily with his fundamental emotions, and so make the least demands upon his intellectual agility, resolution and resourcefulness."

Some years back, just after the stock market had plunged to a nine-year low, T. Rowe Price & Associates, which has had a long history of success as an investment-management firm, issued a bulletin to its private clients that said: "We know from past experience that the best purchases are made when no one else wants stocks and when securities are dumped because the crowd is pessimistic or panicky. At times like these the courage to take a contrary attitude usually pays off."

It's a curious fact of investment life that amateurs are the ones who are the most intent on making the big killing; seasoned professionals are content to make a reasonable return on their investments. Ask a group of average investors if they would be content to make 20 percent a year on their money, and most of them are likely to scoff at what they would describe as a paltry return. But ask them if they would be satisfied with doubling their money in four years or quadrupling it in eight years, and you will undoubtedly get an enthusiastic response. Yet a double in four years and a quadruple in eight is just what you would achieve if you could get a compounded growth rate of 20 percent a year. Most professionals would be delighted to obtain such a return year in and year out. When the market is making a strong bull run, that may not be too hard. But when stocks are plunging, it may be virtually impossible.

The key, then, as Harold B. Ehrlich, chairman emeritus of the investment-management firm of Bernstein-Macaulay, bluntly puts it, is this: "Never take a big loss—ever." Eugene D. Brody, author and options chief at Oppenheimer Capital Corp., points out that if you're seeking a 15 percent compounded return, but you suffer a 10 percent loss, you will need a 47 percent gain the following year to get back on track. And Raymond J. Armstrong, whose Starwood Management Corp. manages investments for some of the most prominent families in America, notes: "Fifty percent up and 50 percent down doesn't leave you in the same place.

For the optimist, the other side of the coin is the knowledge that you can lose only 100 percent of your money, but you can gain an infinite amount. That may be cold comfort, though, for the investor with a limited amount of capital. If he loses that, he may be able to build his stake back only slowly, if at all.

Another crucial piece of advice is to avoid getting stampeded into buying or selling by a sudden event or movement of the market. It's a rare market that doesn't give you a second chance, so don't panic. Prices seldom move straight up or straight down.

Some traders have an uncontrollable desire to be doing something every minute. They feel that unless they're making a trade, they're missing out on important opportunities. But if the trend of the market is in doubt, the best thing to do may be to remain in a neutral position, conserving your cash for the opportune moment. It may not be a bad idea to get out of the market for a time to regain your perspective.

John Train, the author and money manager, says enthusiastic hyperactivity is the hallmark of the losing investor. "The world is not transformed from one day to the next," he points out, "and the average investor makes less money with his brain than what in chess is called his *sitzfleisch*, or patient rear end."

My old *New York Times* colleague Burton Crane, the most respected stock market writer of his day, had this advice: "If you feel scared about the future, get out of the market. A minor speculative turn, later, can make up the income you lost. Unless timidity becomes a habit, there is nothing wrong with having only money."

How many stocks should you own at a time? The pros differ on this. Some advise spreading your risks. On the other hand, Raymond F. DeVoe Jr. of Legg Mason Wood Walker, Inc., one of Wall Street's most literate market analysts, contends that "broad portfolio diversification just spreads the mediocrity." Gerald M. Loeb, stockbroker, market sage, and best-selling author, went both ways on this issue. The beginning investor needs diversification until he learns the ropes, Loeb asserted. But for the professional, he said, "The intelligent and safe way to handle capital is to concentrate." If the market situation is not clear, then do nothing, he counseled. But when something comes up, follow it to the limit, within prudent guidelines. "The greatest safety lies in putting all your eggs in one basket and watching the basket," Loeb added.

My own feeling is somewhere in between. I'd worry about putting all *my* eggs in one basket, no matter how sure I was that I had a winner. What if I were wrong? Or what if some unexpected event—an embargo, a defect, an epidemic, a contract cancellation—threw all my expectations about the company into a cocked hat? Diversifying your portfolio is one way to avoid that.

At the same time, although I generally agree with Mae West that "too much of a good thing can be wonderful," I believe that holding too many stocks is counterproductive. Look at a vaudeville juggler. Even though he gets paid for keeping a lot of balls up in the air at the same time, he's able to pull off that trick for only a short time. How many investors do you know who try to do the same thing with the stocks they own—but fail to recognize the limitations of their concentration and stamina. Don't fall prey to the common mistake of scattering your investments too widely. Most people just cannot follow too many stocks on their own. And by trying to do so, they may not concentrate on the really good ones they've uncovered.

Deciding When to Sell

Sell a stock when it goes down more than 10 percent. You should discipline yourself to sell it and then perhaps look at it again and see if you still would like to buy.
—BARTON BIGGS

How often have you heard the comment, "I can't wait to get even, so I can get out"? What nonsense. It's ridiculous to think that the market knows or cares about the price at which you bought that stock. It means something only to your own ego and psyche. Chances are that the money—and/or the tax loss—you can obtain from selling a losing stock can do a lot more for you than holding on to a dog while you're hoping for it to get you back to where you started. There's also the likelihood that when the stock does recover enough to make you even, it will be in the midst of an upmove that makes it the wrong time to get out. Keep in mind that it's only the value of a stock and its relationship to the rest of the market—at the present moment—that should determine whether you hold on to it or get rid of it.

In talking with top stock market professionals over the years, I've been struck by one nearly unanimous refrain: The biggest mistake most investors make is not knowing when to sell. Deciding what and when to buy is hard enough, but the decision to sell is all too often emotional, quixotic, or put off much too long.

Sigmund Freud once shocked his niece when she asked him for advice on how to make a decision. "Toss a coin," he said. The young woman said she had expected better from him, but he explained that he had not suggested that she follow the coin blindly. "What I want you to do is note what the coin indicates," he said. "Then look into your own reactions. Ask yourself, 'Am I pleased? Am I disappointed?' That will help you recognize how you really feel about the matter deep down inside. Then you will be able to come to a decision."

An experienced trader on the floor of the New York Stock Exchange, who was later to become chairman of the Big Board, once took me on a visit to his frenzied domain. As we walked among the shouting traders and clerks, dodging pages and wading through a litter of discarded paper, he told me how his partner, one of the most highly regarded floor traders on the exchange at that time, operated. "We made a study of his trades," my friend told me, "and we found that 65 percent of the time they were on the losing side." With that record, I inquired, what makes him so great? "Because he knows how to cut his losses," was the reply. "When he buys a stock, he does so with an idea of where he expects it to go. If it goes in the opposite direction, he admits his mistake, sells his stock, and takes the loss. But if it hits his objective and seems to be still moving up, he sells half and rides with the rest. That way, he minimizes his losses and maximizes his gains—at least half of them."

One of the most comprehesive guides to developing a selling strategy based on a technical approach to the market is a book titled *When to Sell* (Farrar, Straus & Giroux, 1972). It's written by two brothers well versed in the intricacies of the market, Justin and Robert Mamis. Robert is an author who regularly writes about the stock market. Justin spent five years as a floor official at the New York Stock Exchange and then founded the highly regarded advisory service called *The Professional Tape Reader,* now operated out of Hollywood, Florida, by his former partner, Stan Weinstein. Since then, Justin has been managing money for the partners of several Wall Street firms and has launched a new bi-weekly stock market letter called *Insights.*

Justin Mamis says he's learned the most about "when to sell" from his experiences as a money manager and consultant to big institutions. The biggest realization, he says, is that "No one ever knows the negatives about a stock in time to sell at the top." Money managers are almost always aware of a company's good news, but it is only the chart action that announces when a top has formed and it is time to sell. Thus, his first rule is: Believe the market action and not the "good" fundamentals. A stock typically makes its top when the news is at its best. Mamis' second rule, therefore, is to sell when a stock no longer advances on good news.

The third guideline has a consistent theme to it: Don't sell until a stock does something wrong. This has its seeds in smart buying. Getting in on a stock near its breakout point is the path to safe buying because that means the support of the base is just underneath. Two things then define the uptrend: (1) the long-term moving average line must be pointing upward; and (2) the stock should move in a series of higher highs and higher lows. By definition, these two factors prove the uptrend.

So long as the stock does not violate either of these two factors, Justin Mamis says, hold it. Give the stock every chance to prove itself. Traders can try to snare their profits if the rise has carried up to a major resistance area (such as from the previous top), but longer term investors should patiently wait until the stock does something wrong. Sooner or later it will fail. The first sign usually is that the next rally fails to make a new high. If the subsequent sell-off carries to a low that is below the previous sell-off, then the sequence has clearly changed to a pattern of lower highs and lower lows—that's a downtrend, and you don't want to own the stock anymore.

The pattern discussed above occurs when the stock begins by doing well. No one is perfect, not even the professionals. If the market is zooming, and your selection languishes, the message is in the weakness. Stocks that don't do what they are supposed to do should be sold.

Lastly, Justin Mamis emphasizes, make sure you place an appropriate stop-loss order. The best time to do this is when you buy the stock because that's when you are "sure" the stop order will never be executed. Therefore, you can be objective. It costs nothing to enter the order, yet it can protect all of your capital. And if the price of the stock is too far above (more than 15 percent, say) where you would place a sensible stop, that in itself is warning that you are buying at too high a price.

Making Stock Market Profits for Absolutely Wrong Reasons

What is actually happening is often less important than what appears to be happening.
—WILLIAM V. SHANNON

Most experienced Wall Streeters have a favorite story about how people have made money in the stock market for the wrong reasons. Sidney Rheinstein, who spent more than fifty years as a floor partner and specialist at the New York Stock Exchange, liked to tell the one about a flamboyant trader of bygone years named J.J. Manning. It was Manning's custom to arrive at the exchange every morning ten minutes before the 10 a.m. opening bell and phone his office to find out how his account stood.

One morning his clerk did not have the figures ready and so allowed the phone to ring without answering it. Finally, Manning got to the clerk, who hastily explained that the phone had been out of order. Manning got so angry he stalked over to the post at which American Telephone & Telegraph stock was being traded and sold several thousand shares short, with the explanation, "I always knew the goddamn company was no good."

Rheinstein said Manning made $2,000 on that quixotic transaction.

The Thursday 3-to-4 Syndrome

Study the past, if you would divine the future.
—CONFUCIUS

Charles M. Lewis, vice president and stock market strategist at Shearson Lehman Brothers, Inc., has been monitoring the Dow Jones Industrial Average for many years. He's found an unusual trading pattern on Thursdays in the final hour of trading on the New York Stock Exchange. On that day of the week, he says, the Dow will be lower at the close (4 p.m.) than it was at 3 p.m. This has happened approximately 75 percent of the time over the last five years.

Lewis offers these five reasons for what he calls the Thursday 3-to-4 Syndrome:

1. Block desk traders and speculators want to close out positions prior to the weekend.

2. Many traders do not work on Fridays.

3. Friday's bids are thin and volume is low.

4. The traders do not want to wait until the very last day of the week.

5. This is a similar pattern to tax-loss selling. The major tax-loss selling is done in November, rather than December, also to avoid last-minute pressures.

Trading Patterns

The only way to get good long-range results is to get good short-term results back to back.
—LEON LEVY

Ever since I came across its first issue back in 1967, I have been thoroughly fascinated by the *Stock Trader's Almanac*. It is packed full of more unusual stock market lore than any other single publication I know of, and I consider it an essential part of any investor's annual store of information. Besides, it's fun to browse through.

Drawing upon his own research and the work of other stock market experts, Yale Hirsch, the *Almanac*'s editor and publisher, has amassed an array of data and investment advice about annual, seasonal, monthly, and even hourly trading patterns and market cycles. The *Almanac* provides a cornucopia of valuable information for investors of all stages of sophistication. Some of the trading patterns that Hirsch has developed are included in this chapter, with his permission. The *Stock Trader's Almanac* is available for $20, plus $2.25 postage and handling, from the Hirsch Organization Inc., Six Deer Trail, Old Tappan, NJ 07675.

A Typical Day in the Market

Stocks tend to fluctuate.
—J.P. MORGAN

Each day in the stock market is a new ballgame. Bullish news may move the market up, bearish news may send it down. Sometimes the market is unaffected by either. Stocks can seesaw violently throughout the day or remain within a very narrow range.

Most hourly fluctuations seem to be random movements, although it is not uncommon for sharp moves in the last hour or two to continue in the same direction the following morning. Also, by examining the hourly prices of the Dow Jones Industrial Average over a period of more than eighteen years (excluding 1969, when the market closed earlier, and the last seven months of 1968, when it operated on a four-day week), a definite composite pattern emerges.

The "typical" market day opens flat at 10 a.m. and rises slightly in the next hour. Weakness sets in around noon as professionals go to lunch. After rallying toward 2 p.m., the market drifts downward the rest of the afternoon.

Looking at Figure 5, you might think that the market spends a good deal more time declining than rising, and you would be right. What is the reason for this paradox, since the market has had an upward bias over the years? It's this: Suppose the market, as measured by the Dow Jones Industrial Average, has a strong opening and is up five points at the start of the day. Then, with each hourly reading, it gives up half a point, right through to the closing bell. What we finally wind up with on the chart is an opening increase and six hourly decreases. What counts more, however, is that the Dow average has gained two points for the day.

FIGURE 5
Market Performance Each Hour of the Day
(November 1963–April 1982)

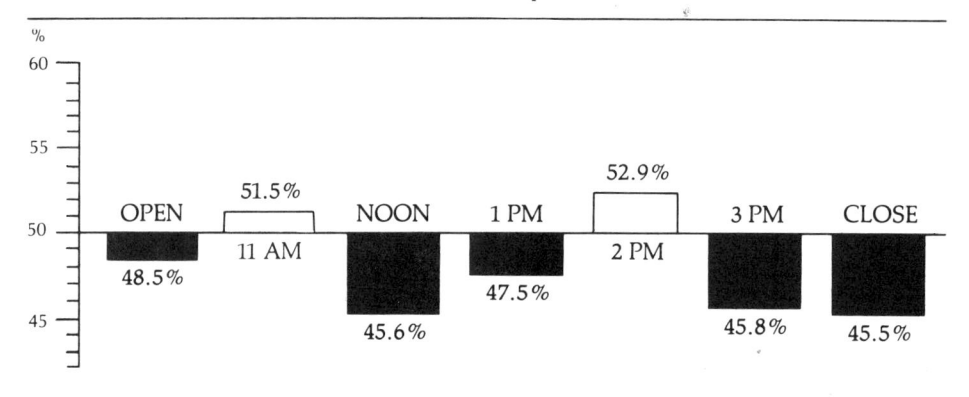

- OPEN: 48.5%
- 11 AM: 51.5%
- NOON: 45.6%
- 1 PM: 47.5%
- 2 PM: 52.9%
- 3 PM: 45.8%
- CLOSE: 45.5%

Based on number of times Dow Jones Industrial Average increased over previous hour.
(Source: *Stock Trader's Almanac,* Yale Hirsch)

The Week's Trading, Hour by Hour

*I've been rich and I've been poor.
Rich is better.*
—Sophie Tucker

Figure 6 shows the percentage of times the Dow Jones Industrial Average rose over the preceding hour (November 1963–April 1982*) the typical week unfolds.

FIGURE 6
Hour by Hour, Through the Week

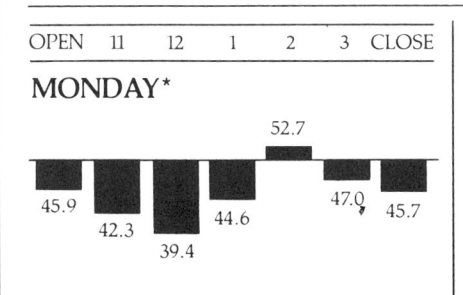

MONDAY*

OPEN 11 12 1 2 3 CLOSE

45.9 | 42.3 | 39.4 | 44.6 | 52.7 | 47.0 | 45.7

Some strength at opening due to impact of usual Monday morning stock recommendations in market letters and reports in Sunday financial sections. Specialists supply the demand by going short. Market drifts lower the rest of the day except for rally near 2 p.m.

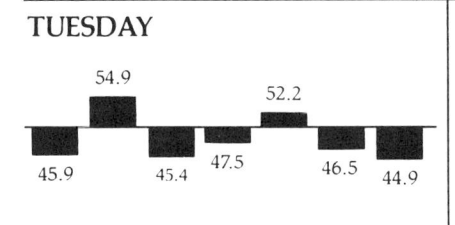

TUESDAY

45.9 | 54.9 | 45.4 | 47.5 | 52.2 | 46.5 | 44.9

Previous day's weakness carries over to opening. Rally later in morning subsides at lunchtime. Rally then resumes quietly until 3 p.m. and sells off at close.

(Figure Continued)

STOCK MARKET SECRETS • 169

WEDNESDAY 49.5 54.0 49.0 49.2 54.7 46.0 44.0	Duplicates previous day's pattern, except for slightly more strength at opening and at lunchhour and a weaker close.
THURSDAY 51.2 53.8 45.7 49.1 53.3 43.1 41.0	Strong in morning, weak at lunchtime, rally near 2 p.m., sell off for weakest close of week.
FRIDAY* 49.9 52.5 48.3 46.9 51.4 48.5 51.7	Strength in morning subsides around lunchtime. Rally then resumes and continues for the strongest close of the week. The traditional Friday afternoon sell-off of former years, as traders lightened holdings prior to the weekend, seems to have been reversed.

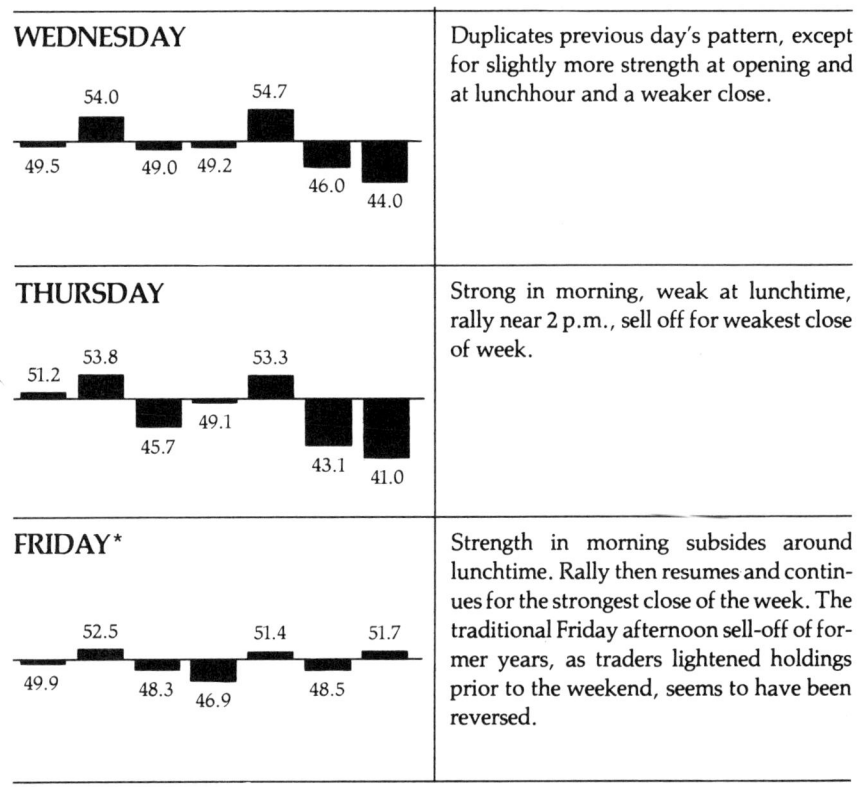

*Research indicates that where Tuesday is the first trading day of the week, it follows the Monday pattern. Therefore, all such Tuesdays were combined with the Mondays here. Thursdays which are the final trading day of a given week behave like Fridays, and were similarly grouped with Fridays.

(**Source:** *Stock Trader's Almanac,* Yale Hirsch)

Fridays Rise More Than Mondays

Money is always there but the pockets change.
—GERTRUDE STEIN

A most unusual phenomenon in the stock market is the startling contrast between the first and last trading days of the week. A tabulation of all trading days in the 30-year period from June 1952 to April 1982 reveals that the first trading day of the week (this can be Tuesday when Monday is a holiday) has a rising market only 42.9 percent of the time. Conversely, the strongest day of the week is the last trading day (this can be Thursday when Friday is a holiday), when the market closes higher 58.7 percent of the time, as illustrated in Figure 7.

Friday's activity has a profound effect on the following Monday's markets, as discovered by Frank Cross of Niederhoffer, Cross & Zeckhauser. When the market is down on Friday, chances are three to one that the following Monday will also decline. During the 1952–1982 period, only 24.8 percent of the Mondays were able to rise after declining Fridays. However, a cluster of three or four "up" Mondays following "down" Fridays occurred around important market bottoms in 1966, 1968, 1970, 1973, and 1974, a point that's considered highly significant as a clue to a market turnaround.

FIGURE 7
Market Performance Each Day of the Week
(June 1952–April 1982)

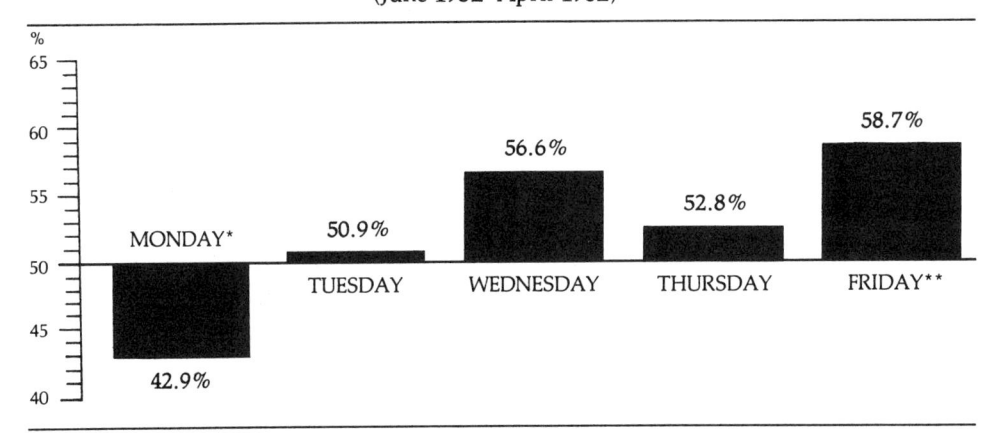

%
- MONDAY*: 42.9%
- TUESDAY: 50.9%
- WEDNESDAY: 56.6%
- THURSDAY: 52.8%
- FRIDAY**: 58.7%

Based on number of times Standard & Poor's composite index closed higher than previous day.

*On Monday holidays, the following Tuesday is included in the Monday figure.
**On Friday holidays, the preceding Thursday is included in the Friday figure.

(Source: *Stock Trader's Almanac*, Yale Hirsch)

Daily Performance Each Year: 1952–1983

Although it cannot be avoided, the unexpected can at least be incorporated into the decision-making process.
—ARTHUR ZEIKEL

In order to determine whether market trend alters the performance of the different days of the week, Yale Hirsch separated the eleven bear-market years of 1953, 1957, 1960, 1962, 1966, 1969, 1970, 1973, 1974, 1977, and 1981 from the twenty-one bull-market years. Although the middle days of the week—Tuesday, Wednesday, and Thursday—did not vary much on average between bull- and bear-market years, Mondays and Fridays were sharply affected by changes in market climate. There was a swing of 12.8 percentage points in performance on Mondays and 12.6 percentage points on Fridays, as shown in Table 1.

TABLE 1
Percentage of Times Market Closed Higher Than Previous Day
(Based on S&P composite index, 1952–1983)

Year	Monday	Tuesday	Wednesday	Thursday	Friday
1952	50.0%	57.7%	56.7%	61.5%	65.5%
1953	32.7	47.9	54.9	60.8	56.6
1954	51.9	57.4	63.5	60.0	73.1
1955	48.1	45.7	67.3	60.8	80.8
1956	34.0	40.0	44.9	50.0	61.5
1957	25.0	58.0	64.7	46.8	46.2
1958	59.6	53.1	59.6	68.1	73.1
1959	40.4	51.0	58.3	51.0	69.2
1960	36.5	52.2	44.2	56.3	61.5
1961	53.8	54.3	62.0	54.0	64.2
1962	28.3	52.1	58.0	51.0	50.0
1963	46.2	63.3	51.0	57.4	69.2
1964	40.4	48.0	62.7	59.6	78.8
1965	46.2	52.1	55.8	51.0	69.2
1966	36.5	47.8	53.8	42.0	57.7
1967	40.4	52.2	58.8	64.0	63.5
1968*	39.1	65.0	60.9	45.0	56.5
1969	32.1	46.9	50.0	67.4	52.8
1970	38.5	44.0	63.5	46.8	51.9
1971	44.2	62.5	55.8	50.0	55.8
1972	38.5	60.4	55.8	51.0	67.3
1973	30.8	51.1	52.9	44.9	42.3
1974	34.6	56.3	52.0	38.8	34.6
1975	53.8	38.8	59.6	58.3	57.7
1976	55.8	56.5	55.8	40.8	56.6
1977	40.4	40.4	46.2	53.1	55.8
1978	51.9	43.5	59.6	54.0	48.1
1979	54.7	51.0	58.8	66.0	44.2
1980	57.6	56.2	69.8	33.3	59.6
1981	46.2	38.8	53.8	54.2	46.2
1982	44.2	39.6	44.2	46.0	48.1
1983	52.0	46.8	59.6	51.0	55.8
Average	43.3%	50.6%	56.7%	53.0%	58.5%
21 Bull Years	47.8%	52.1%	58.1%	53.9%	62.8%
11 Bear Years	34.7%	48.7%	54.0%	51.1%	50.5%

*Excludes last six months of four-day market weeks.
(Source: *Stock Trader's Almanac*, Yale Hirsch)

The Best Days of the Month

You can't expect to hit the jackpot if you don't put a few nickels in the machine.
—FLIP WILSON

The market rises more often (61.4 percent) on the second trading day of the month than on any other. And a period of five consecutive trading days—the last, first, second, third, and fourth trading days of the month—distinctly outperforms the trading days in the rest of the month. In a 360-month study (May 1952–April 1982), the market was up 57.8 percent of the time on these five bullish days compared with an average of 52.5 percent for the remaining sixteen trading days of a typical month (see Figure 8).

This trading pattern occurs because most investors, individuals as well as institutions, tend to operate on a monthly fiscal basis. Consequently, the big cash inflows at banks, funds, and insurance companies around the end or beginning of the month often cause upward pressures due to simultaneous purchase decisions.

Much of the market strength in the 30 years studied has occurred around the last plus the first four trading days of the month. While the market has risen on the average 52.5 percent of the time, the prime five days have risen 57.8 percent.

Sophisticated short-term traders, floor specialists, and portfolio managers could benefit immensely by studying this month-end/beginning upward bias and perhaps devising some seat-of-the-pants trading strategy. It would be difficult, though, for long-term investors to take advantage of this far-from-random phenomenon.

There is no pat formula for instant riches here. Nevertheless, there have been many occasions at month's end when the market has paused during a sharp downturn and then spurted upward after a resting or quiet phase, or when it has accelerated its previously gradual rate of climb during a bull market.

FIGURE 8
Market Performance Each Day of the Month
(May 1952–April 1982)

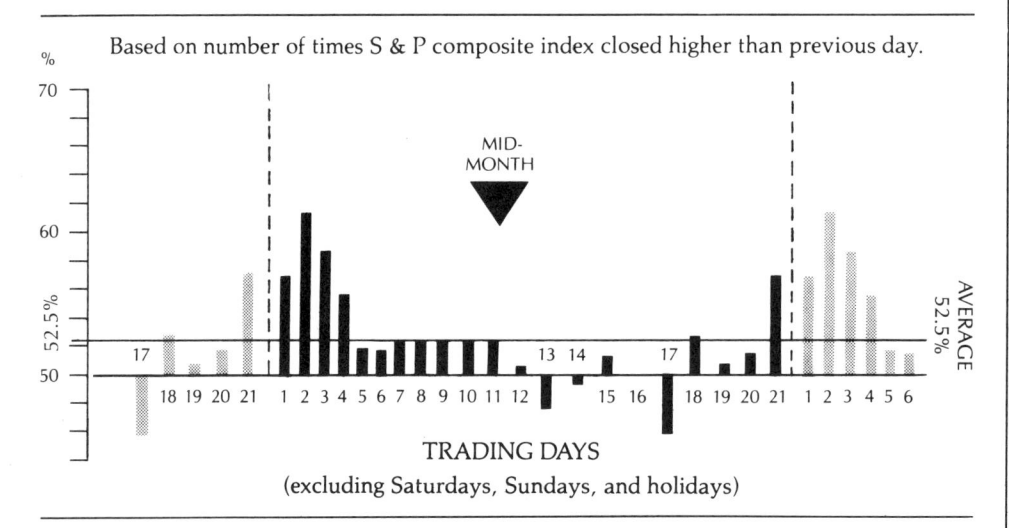

Based on number of times S & P composite index closed higher than previous day.

TRADING DAYS
(excluding Saturdays, Sundays, and holidays)

(Source: *Stock Trader's Almanac*, Yale Hirsch)

176 • HOW TO BEAT WALL STREET

The Best Months of the Year

October. This is one of the peculiarly dangerous months to speculate in stocks. Others are November, December, January, February, March, April, May, June, July, August and September.
—MARK TWAIN

The most important observation to be made from Figure 9, which shows the average monthly change in market prices since 1951, is that institutions —mutual funds, pension funds, banks, and the like—determine the trading patterns in today's market.

The "investment calendar" reflects the annual, semiannual, and quarterly operations of institutions during January, April, and July. October is the one exception. Besides being a "tight money" month, a time for portfolio tax switching, the beginning of the new car year, and the last campaign month before elections, October is also the time when most bear markets seem to end, as they did in 1946, 1957, 1960, 1962, 1966, and 1974.

The year-end strength in November and December is probably influenced greatly by the fast-growing corporate and private pension funds. Most of them receive new investment funds in a lump sum once a year, producing a lopsided effect in the year-end market.

Between 1934 and 1949, when the market stayed within the 100 to 200 range in the Dow Jones Industrial Average, January, June, July, and October stood out as the strongest months of the year. It is obvious that a decided shift in investment seasons has occurred in recent years.

FIGURE 9
Market Performance Each Month of the Year
34½ Years (Jan. 1950–Jun. 1984)

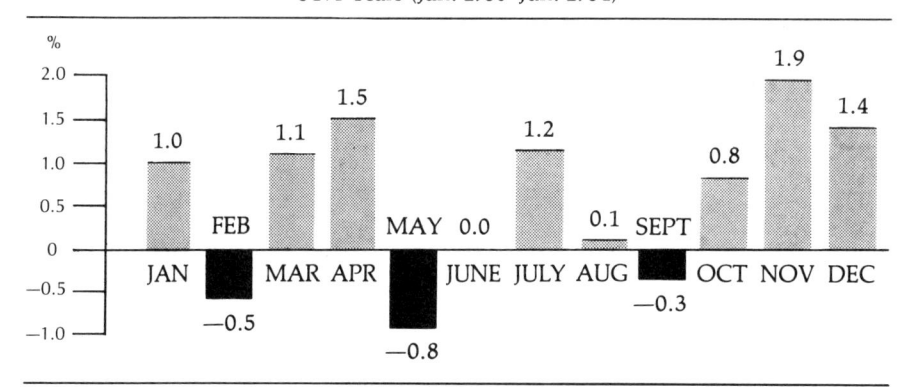

Month	%
JAN	1.0
FEB	−0.5
MAR	1.1
APR	1.5
MAY	−0.8
JUNE	0.0
JULY	1.2
AUG	0.1
SEPT	−0.3
OCT	0.8
NOV	1.9
DEC	1.4

Average month-to-month % change in Standard & Poor's composite index
(Based on monthly closing prices)

(Source: *Stock Trader's Almanac,* Yale Hirsch)

How the Super Bowl Forecasts the Stock Market

The game is old, but the players are always new!
—FRED C. KELLY

Although the parallel between professional football and the stock market may be difficult for fundamentalists to grasp, there is a distinct correlation between the outcome of nearly every Super Bowl championship game since January 1967 and that year's performance of the Standard & Poor's 500 index.

Prior to the merger of the National Football League with the American Football League in the late 1960s, there were sixteen teams in the NFL and ten teams in the AFL. To facilitate the merger and have two conferences of equal size, three teams from the old NFL—Pittsburgh, Baltimore, and Cleveland—were added to the ten original teams from the AFL to form the new American Football Conference, making it the same size as the new National Football Conference. Each had thirteen teams.

Robert H. Stovall, director of investment policy at Dean Witter Reynolds, Inc., developed the Super Bowl Market Predictor.

In the eighteen Super Bowls played since the first one in 1967, whenever the National Football Conference (or an "old" NFL team now in the American Football Conference, such as Pittsburgh or Baltimore) entrant won, that year's Standard & Poor's 500 went up. As can be seen in Table 2, this bullish result occurred eleven times: 1967, 1968, 1971, 1972, 1975, 1976, 1978, 1979, 1980, 1982 and 1983. Conversely, when one of the AFL teams won, as was the case in 1969, 1973, 1974, 1977, and 1981, the S&P 500 usually declined that year. The only exceptions in this series occurred in 1970 when Kansas City (an original AFL team) won, and the S&P 500 went *up* 0.1 percent, and 1984, when the Los Angeles Raiders (formerly the Oakland Raiders, another former AFL team) won, and the S&P went *up* 1.4 percent (although the Dow Jones industrials did go *down*). According to the Super Bowl Stock Market Predictor Theory, the S&P should have declined both those years.

Thus, in sixteen of the eighteen Super Bowls played through 1984, or 88.9 percent of the time, the Super Bowl Predictor has correctly forecast the course of the S&P 500 for the year that would end some eleven months later. So, if you're bullish on the stock market, root for the boys from the NFL to win. If you're a bear, root for the AFL team.

TABLE 2
Super Bowl Market Predictor

Super Bowl Number	Year	Winner	League	S&P 500 12/31 Previous Year	Close 12/31 Current Year	Percent Change
I	1967	GREEN BAY	NFL	80.33	96.47	+20.1%
II	1968	GREEN BAY	NFL	96.47	103.86	+ 7.7%
III	1969	N.Y. JETS	AFL	103.86	92.06	−11.4%
IV	1970	KANSAS CITY	AFL	92.06	92.15	+ 0.1%**
V	1971	BALTIMORE	AFL*	92.15	102.09	+10.8%
VI	1972	DALLAS	NFL	102.09	118.05	+15.6%
VII	1973	MIAMI	AFL	118.05	97.55	−17.4%
VIII	1974	MIAMI	AFL	97.55	68.56	−29.7%
IX	1975	PITTSBURGH	AFL*	68.56	90.19	+31.5%
X	1976	PITTSBURGH	AFL*	90.19	107.46	+19.1%
XI	1977	OAKLAND	AFL	107.46	95.10	−11.5%
XII	1978	DALLAS	NFL	95.10	96.11	+ 1.1%
XIII	1979	PITTSBURGH	NFL	96.11	107.94	+12.3%
XIV	1980	PITTSBURGH	AFL*	107.94	135.76	+25.8%
XV	1981	OAKLAND	AFL	135.76	122.55	− 9.7%
XVI	1982	SAN FRANCISCO	NFL	122.55	140.64	+14.8%
XVII	1983	WASHINGTON	NFL	140.64	163.55	+17.3%
XVIII	1984	L.A./OAKLAND	AFL	163.55	167.24	+ 1.4%**
XIX	1985	SAN FRANCISCO	NFL	167.24	-	-

*Formerly NFL.
**Sole exceptions to date.
(Source: William LeFerre, Purcell, Graham & Co.)

Stock Market Advice Can Have a Comic Flavor

The public? How many fools does it take to make a public?
—CHAMFORT

Stock market prognosticators sometimes base their forecasts on unusual sources of information. Some use elaborate charts or computer printouts; others analyze patterns of trading by corporate insiders; still others rely on the stars. One of the most remarkable systems was devised by Frederick N. Goldsmith, whose market letter, first published in 1916, developed an ardent following over a period of more than thirty years.

Eventually, when Goldsmith was in his eighties, the New York State Attorney General and the Securities and Exchange Commission cracked down on him and in the process revealed how he had "cracked" the code of the big-time market traders. The key, he explained, could be found in the then popular *Bringing Up Father* comic strip, which featured a character named Jiggs. If Jiggs was pictured with his right hand in his pocket, the market was a buy. If he was shown with two puffs of smoke rising from his cigar, this meant that the market would be strong in the second hour of trading. Goldsmith explained that when one strip showed Jiggs, at the theater, observing, "The intermissions are the only good thing about this show," Goldsmith advised his subscribers to buy Mission Oil (which went up 15 points the next day). As outlandish as all this sounds, top Wall Street brokers and some big investors testified that they followed Goldsmith's advice and found him to be remarkably accurate.

Goldsmith himself testified: "Since the year 1900, I have been able to call with absolute accuracy every top and bottom of every long swing that has been made [in the market] from that time until now."

Nevertheless, the judge hearing the case barred him from the business with this comment: "The subscribers to the defendant's daily market letter had the right to assume that the defendant possessed a superior knowledge of the stock market, that whatever information he had came from living persons and recognized sources and not as a result of interpretations of comic strips. When he failed to inform his subscribers of the alleged sources of information, he was concealing a material fact."

One of the prosecutors in the case added: "This should give rise to serious reflection on the part of the public as to the actual value of many stock market forecasts."

Long-Lasting Nuggets of Wall Street Wisdom

Life is just one damn thing after another.
—ELBERT HUBBARD

The stock market is full of fads and theories that sometimes seem as changeable as this year's fashions. But many verities of investment wisdom have endured for scores of years and even through the centuries. A list of them was put together in the early 1960s by Paul Sarnoff, a broker, analyst, and prolific Wall Street writer. Go through this list and see how many of those legendary gems of wisdom still hold true today.

1. Pay bills first...then buy stocks.

2. Do not speculate with other people's money.

3. Don't neglect your business for wine, women, or stocks.

4. Never regret a stock market move.

5. Don't make the same mistake...twice.

6. Take no advice from the uninformed.

7. To profit from informed advice you need...luck.

8. You can never outguess the market.

9. The market never does what the experts think it will do.

10. The public is always wrong.

11. Never sell on strike news.

12. Buy on weakness...sell on strength.

13. Don't wait for a top or bottom...profit in-between.

14. Never overextend yourself.

15. The bulls make money; the bears make money; the hogs lose.

16. Don't go partners with anyone in stock market trades.

17. Discretion given is control lost.

18. Investigate before you invest...then get lucky.

19. Don't put all your investment eggs in one basket.

20. Good stocks recover; cats and dogs die.

21. Only risk part of your reserves in the market.

22. Never be in a hurry to buy or sell.

23. It is always easier for the public to buy than sell.

24. The market is most dangerous at its best...and at its best when at its worst.

25. Never pyramid without protection.

26. Watch the news and then....act.

27. If you speculate and win...then invest.

28. Learn from your errors.

29. An easy buck is hard to make...in Wall Street.

30. Base your market decisions on the intelligent application of facts...not emotion.

31. There is always something left after taxes...if you have profits.

32. People who can't afford to lose shouldn't play the market.

33. If stocks don't rise...they'll decline.

34. All stocks are bought to be sold.

35. *Caveat emptor* was not only for Romans.

36. You can never go broke taking small profits (your broker will get rich).

37. The most valuable asset in Wall Street is information, but to profit, you also need...luck.

38. The best way to swear secrecy...is not to tell.

39. A small, real loss often prevents a large, paper one.

40. A well-bought stock is half sold.

41. Never buy stocks you can't watch.

42. Never buy from strangers...know your broker.

43. No one knows which way the market or a stock will go. If they did, they would tell no one and be content to reap their own fortune.

44. A fool and his money are soon parted...in life and also in the market.

45. Since the profit or loss will be yours...the investment decisions should also be yours.

46. Stocks, like children, need watching!

47. Always sell on news (except strike news).

48. Be guided by reason, not rumor.

49. Never wait for that extra eighth.

50. When you are in doubt about a stock...do nothing.

51. Today's closing prices may never appear tomorrow.

52. Plan the prudent employment of your money.

53. You can't fool the tape.

54. Never buck a trend.

55. Don't go short stock you can't borrow.

56. Never sell a call without owning the stock.

57. Never sell a put unless you are prepared to buy the stock.

58. Never sell a straddle unless you have protected one side...and have the funds to protect the other side.

59. A late tape causes quick losses.

60. It takes more intelligence to profit from good advice than to give it.

61. Nimble speculators may make money by acting against the public.

62. Every stock market has its day...never overstay it.

63. If you want to buy—buy. If you want to sell—sell. But learn how to protect yourself.

64. The most risk often brings the least reward.

65. Tips are only as good as their sources.

66. Before you buy, determine who you can sell to.

67. The record of a mutual fund's performance is no criterion of future performance.

68. Charts are primarily used for recording the past.

69. People who spend millions to learn how to profit in the market... won't spend pennies to learn protection.

Appendix

Appendix: The Wise Men and Women of Wall Street —And Where to Find Them

Stefan Abrams is a managing director of Oppenheimer & Co., Inc., and chairman of the stock-selection committee. He started his Wall Street career in 1962 as an analyst with Loeb, Rhoades & Co., served as vice president and portfolio manager of the Abacus Fund, and joined Oppenheimer in 1973. He has been chairman of the stock-selection committee since 1978.

Oppenheimer & Co., Inc., One New York Plaza, New York, N.Y. 10004.

Mark J. Appleman is a former Wall Street executive who now is a management consultant in the field of investor relations. He is also publisher of *The Corporate Shareholder,* a biweekly newsletter on the subject, and publishes special reports for corporate managements. He is the author of seven books on investment topics, as well as a Hollywood film, a Broadway play, and a novel.

The Corporate Shareholder, 271 Madison Avenue, New York, N.Y. 10016.

Hans J. Baer is president of the management committee of Bank Julius Baer & Co., Ltd., of Zurich, Switzerland, and chairman of the Julius Baer Group, the holding company that directs the bank's international operations. He lived in the United States for many years, receiving a bachelor's degree in engineering from Lehigh University and a master's degree in economics from New York University. He has been a visiting fellow at both Oxford and Harvard Universities.

Bank Julius Baer & Co., Ltd., Bahnhofstrasse 36, Postfach 8022, Zurich, Switzerland.

James Balog is senior executive vice president of Drexel Burnham Lambert, Inc., with responsibility for the firm's research, investment advisory division, and Middle East business development. During his twenty-four-year Wall Street career, he has been a securities analyst, portfolio manager, director of research, and head of institutional sales and trading. He was chairman of William D. Witter when it merged with Drexel Burnham Lambert in 1976.

Drexel Burnham Lambert, Inc., 60 Broad Street, New York, N.Y. 10004.

Ann C. Brown came to Wall Street after a successful career as a Madison Avenue advertising executive and a private investor. She joined the institutional research firm of Baker, Weeks & Co. in 1969 and in 1977 co-founded the investment firm of Melhado, Flynn & Associates, where she served as executive vice president. Now she heads A.C. Brown & Associates, a private stock market consulting firm, and is a regular stock market columnist for *Forbes* magazine.

Forbes, 60 Fifth Avenue, New York, N.Y. 10011.

Eugene D. Brody is a senior vice president of Oppenheimer Capital Corp. and director of the Option Management Division. He began his Wall Street career in 1957 at Eastman, Dillion, Union Securities and subsequently founded his own option-writing firm. He later became a general partner of A.W. Jones & Co. and chief executive officer of Founders Mutual Deposit Corp., which managed mutual funds and other investment accounts. In 1975 he joined Oppenheimer & Co., Inc., and became special

partner in charge of the firm's option activities.
Oppenheimer Capital Corp., One New York Plaza, New York, N.Y. 10004.

Louis Ehrenkrantz is a former high school English teacher who became a stockbroker and brokerage house executive. In 1973, he co-founded Rosenkrantz, Ehrenkrantz, Lyon & Ross, Inc. Since early 1985, he has been a director of Ehrenkrantz & King, the research arm of Reich & Co. A manager of investment portfolios for more than twenty years, he also is the author of three investment letters published by his company: *Investing for Growth, Undiscovered Equities,* and *Investing and Technology.*
Ehrenkrantz & King, 50 Broadway, New York, N.Y. 10004.

Harold B. Ehrlich is chairman emeritus and former chief executive officer of Bernstein-Macaulay, Inc., which manages investment portfolios totaling more than $8 billion. He is also a senior executive vice president of Shearson Lehman Brothers, Inc. In his twenty-seven years in the investment industry, he has been a securities analyst, director of research and portfolio manager. He holds a doctorate in economics and has written and lectured widely on economic and investment subjects. He is also a co-founder of Computer Science Capital, Ltd., which creates companies engaged in the development of computer software.
Bernstein-Macaulay, Inc., 505 Park Avenue, New York, N.Y. 10022.

Monte J. Gordon, vice president and director of research of the Dreyfus Corporation, is one of the most widely quoted men on Wall Street. He began his investment career thirty-seven years ago as an analyst with Bache & Co., and during his twenty-four years with that firm held the posts of research director, senior vice president in charge of marketing, sales and product coordination, and chairman of the investment policy board. He joined the Dreyfus Corporation, which now manages funds to-

taling $25 billion, as director of research in 1972.
Dreyfus Corporation, 767 Fifth Avenue, New York, N.Y. 10153.

William R. Hambrecht is a senior partner of the brokerage and investment banking firm of Hambrecht & Quist. He started in the investment business as a broker in 1958 and ten years later co-founded his present firm, which specializes in investment banking and venture capital activities in the high-technology field. He currently serves as a director of a dozen publicly held corporations.
Hambrecht & Quist, 235 Montgomery Street, San Francisco C.A. 94104.

Yale Hirsch is best known as the publisher of the *Stock Trader's Almanac,* which is now in its eighteenth edition. For the last eleven years he has also been the editor and publisher of *Smart Money,* a monthly investment newsletter whose leading feature is a section titled "America's Most Undiscovered Companies." He is the author of the *Directory of Exceptional Stockbrokers,* which his company published in 1982.
The Hirsch Organization, 6 Deer Trail, Old Tappan, N.J. 07675.

Lucien O. Hopper is vice president of Thomson McKinnon Securities, a major Wall Street brokerage house. He is the author of a stock market letter that has appeared regularly since 1922, and he has served as president of the New York Society of Security Analysts and of the Financial Analysts Federation.
Thomson McKinnon Securities Inc., One New York Plaza, New York, N.Y. 10004.

George S. Johnson is president and chief executive officer of Scudder, Stevens & Clark, the nation's largest independent investment counseling firm, which he joined upon his graduation from Yale in 1948. He and his firm have been among the leading innovators in the investment field, having launched in the United States the first international, dual-purpose, and special mutual funds.

Scudder, Stevens & Clark, 345 Park Avenue, New York, N.Y. 10154.

Michael J. Johnston is president of Paine Webber Capital Markets, which includes the investment banking, fixed income, institutional equities, and financial institutions and markets divisions of Paine Webber, Inc. He began his investment career as a mutual fund securities analyst in 1964. Three years later he joined Mitchel Hutchins, Inc., as an analyst following technological industries and he became director of investment research in 1970.

Paine Webber Capital Markets, 1285 Avenue of the Americas, New York, N.Y. 10019.

David M. Jones is senior vice president and chief economist of Aubrey G. Lanston & Co., a leading Wall Street dealer in government securities. He spent five years at the Federal Reserve Bank of New York, as economist and head of the business forecasting section and on the domestic bond-trading desk. After five years as financial economist of Irving Trust Co., he joined Aubrey G. Lanston as editor of its weekly letter. He is one of Wall Street's best-known Fed-watchers and money market forecasters.

Aubrey G. Lanston & Co., 20 Broad Street, New York, N.Y. 10005.

Jean M. Kirk is a vice president and communications coordinator of T. Rowe Price Associates, Inc., which manages more than $17 billion in mutual funds and other investment accounts. As communications director, she is responsible for providing market intelligence and information about national economic and political trends to the firm's investment decision-makers. Before joining T. Rowe Price in 1969, she worked for Alex Brown & Sons.

T. Rowe Price Associates, Inc., 100 East Pratt Street, Baltimore MD. 21202.

Bernard J. Lasker is senior partner of Lasker, Stone & Stern, a specialist firm on the floor of the New York Stock Exchange. He started his Wall Street career as a runner in 1927, bought a Big Board seat in 1939, and cofounded his present firm eight years later. He served as chairman of the New York Stock Exchange in 1969–1970 and helped steer the exchange through its most difficult period in recent history.
Lasker, Stone & Stern, 20 Broad Street, New York, N.Y. 10005.

William M. LeFevre is vice president and investment strategist of the brokerage firm of Purcell, Graham & Co. In his twenty-eight years on Wall Street, he has been a floor partner on the New York Stock Exchange, a securities analyst, a research director, and an investment strategist. For the last eleven years, he has written the widely-read *Monday Morning Market Letter.*
Purcell, Graham & Co., 61 Broadway, New York, N.Y. 10006.

Charles M. Lewis is a vice president of Shearson Lehman Brothers, Inc., and a widely quoted expert on stock market movements. He started in the securities industry in 1959 as a registered representative with Hirsch & Co. He served as the managing partner of Treves & Co. and joined Shearson in 1979.
Shearson Lehman Brothers, Inc., 767 Fifth Avenue, New York, N.Y. 10153.

Robert B. Menschel is a limited partner of Goldman, Sachs & Co., which he joined thirty years ago. He was a founder of the firm's institutional department and served as partner in charge of institutional sales for twelve years. He has a reputation of being one of Wall Street's most consistently successful investors.
Goldman, Sachs & Co., 85 Broad Street, New York, N.Y. 10004.

Eric T. Miller is chief investment policy officer and a senior vice president of Donaldson, Lufkin & Jenrette, Inc. During his thirty-two years on Wall Street, he has served as a portfolio manager, head of investment management and director of research. Before joining Donaldson, Lufkin & Jenrette in 1979, he was a vice president and chairman of the investment policy committee of Oppenheimer & Co., Inc.

Donaldson, Lufkin & Jenrette, Inc., 140 Broadway, New York, N.Y. 10005.

Arnold X. Moskowitz is senior vice president and economist of Dean Witter Reynolds, Inc., responsible for forecasting the economy, analyzing government economic policy, and presenting equity and credit market forecasts. Before joining the firm as associate economist in 1970, he was an analyst with the Grumman Corp. He has written widely on the subjects of interest rates, Federal Reserve policy, the stock market, and portfolio management.

Dean Witter Reynolds, Inc., 5 World Trade Center, New York, N.Y. 10048.

Pierre A. Rinfret is president and chief executive officer of Rinfret Associates, an international economic, financial and political intelligence firm whose clients include leading business and financial organizations. Known for his outspoken and independent economic views, he has counseled three Presidents—John F. Kennedy, Lyndon B. Johnson, and Richard M. Nixon—and served as principal economic spokesman for Mr. Nixon's 1972 presidential campaign. Prior to founding his own firm in 1967, he spent fifteen years with Lionel D. Edie & Co., economic and investment counselors, joining as a staff economist and rising to chairman.

Rinfret Associates Inc., 641 Lexington Avenue, New York, N.Y. 10022.

Martin D. Sass is chairman and president of M.D. Sass Investor Services Inc., and American Management Enterprises, Inc. investment-management companies managing assets of more than $1.5 billion. Prior to forming these companies in 1972, he was president of Neuwirth Management Corp. and founder and director of the Argus Research special situations division.

M.D. Sass Investors Services, Inc., 475 Park Avenue South, New York, N.Y. 10016.

Robert H. Stovall is senior vice president and director of investment policy for Dean Witter Reynolds, Inc. He began his Wall Street career as a messenger for Reynolds & Co. in 1940, and with time out for two university degrees and military service during World War II, has been in the investment business ever since. He's been a securities and market analyst for thirty years and has been a partner or voting stockholder of a major New York Stock Exchange member firm since 1961.

Dean Witter Reynolds, Inc., 1 World Trade Center, New York, N.Y. 10048.

Donald I. Trott has been a Wall Street analyst and research director for more than two decades. He started his business career as a petroleum analyst in the investment research department of Chase Manhattan bank. From 1967 to 1976 he was research director and chairman of Jas. H. Oliphant & Co., a brokerage firm noted for its institutional research. He was chairman of the investment policy committee of A.G. Becker, Inc., and now is director of research of Mabon, Nugent & Co.

Mabon, Nugent & Co., 115 Broadway, New York, N.Y. 10006.

John Westergaard is president, editor and publisher of Equity Research Associates, Inc., an investment advisory subsidiary of Ladenburg, Thalmann & Co., Inc., members of the New York Stock Exchange. He is also president of the Westergaard Fund, Inc., a growth stock-oriented mutual fund started in 1983. He started in the investment business in 1957 and co-founded Equity Research Associates in 1962. Over the years, he has become known as one of Wall Street's most articulate proponents of investing in junior growth stocks.

Equity Research Associates, Inc., 540 Madison Avenue, New York, N.Y. 10022.

Arthur Williams III is vice president for pension fund investment of Merrill Lynch & Co., Inc., responsible for the investment of the $450 million in the pension fund of Merrill Lynch's own employees. He also manages special investments for the company's key executives and acts as an adviser to major pension and endowment funds. He first came to Wall Street in 1964 as a securities analyst and joined Merrill Lynch in 1974 as a performance measurement specialist.

Merrill Lynch & Co., One Liberty Plaza, New York, N.Y. 10080.

About the Author

Myron Kandel is one of the country's best-known financial editors, writers, and broadcasters. He helped start Cable News Network, the 24-hour, all-news television network, which went on the air in June, 1980, and has served since then as CNN's financial editor and economics analyst.

He has also been the financial editor of three major newspapers: the *New York Herald Tribune,* the *Washington Star,* and the *New York Post.* He was editor of the *New York Law Journal* and also founded and served as editor and publisher of several newsletters, including *The Wall Street Letter* and *Review of the Financial Press.* For nearly eight years, he co-authored a nationally syndicated financial column, *The Greer/Kandel Report,* which appeared in leading papers across the country.

He has also combined practical business experience with his career as a working journalist. After selling *The Wall Street Letter* to Institutional Investor Systems, Inc., he became executive vice president of that publishing company, and while editing the *New York Law Journal,* he also served as president of the company that published the nation's largest daily legal newspaper.

Starting his journalism career as a copyboy on *The New York Times,* he worked as a copy editor and financial reporter for that newspaper; as a foreign correspondent and then financial editor of the *New York Herald Tribune,* and as a Washington correspondent for Armed Forces Press Service.

He is a graduate of Brooklyn College and the Columbia Graduate School of Journalism and has taught journalism at Columbia and at the City College of New York. He is a former president of the Society of American Business and Economic Writers; of the Deadline Club chapter of the Society of Professional Journalists/Sigma Delta Chi, and of the Alumni Association of the Columbia Graduate School of Journalism. He is presently vice president of the New York Financial Writers Association.